Disaster Preparedness

For When It Is Not the End of the World.

By

Dr. Disaster

Table of Contents

AHHHHHH!
Hey, this isn't so hard
The most important prep
What to do now to feel ready
Get the basics first: Food
Water: It's not just for swimming in
Security: The bad guys kill too
Shelter: It's got you covered
Energy runs your world
Self Reliance is a lifestyle
Debt kills the future, savings saves it
Alternative investments
Thoughts concerning health
Fear: The wrong reason to prepare
Do you need a bunker?
The single event to prepare for
Common natural disasters
Closing thoughts

AHHHHHH!

Lots of folks worry about *the end of the world as we know it* (TEOTWAWKI); I say they worry about the wrong thing. The world will not end. Rather than worry about TEOTWAWKI, they should be worried about the end of the world as **they** know it.

Have you ever lost a job that you relied on to meet the bills? Maybe it was a really good job that paid well enough that one spouse could decide to stay home and pursue other important things. When you, or someone you know lost that job, I'll wager to myself to eat my own hat, that you felt like it was the end of the world as **you** knew it.

Have you, or someone you know ever been injured or sick to such a degree that income was affected. I do not refer to the medical bills sucking away your income, although it hurts; I mean that you could not go to work for an extended time, beyond the time that some employers offer sick pay. A time frame of six months or more without work and the income it provides. Maybe that leads to the loss of the job too. Did it feel like the end of your world?

The end of the world is a pretty serious thing; but the end of **your** world is just as serious because it happens to you. Millions of people all over the world experience the end of their world as they know it, everyday. Job loss, injury, weather, war, economics, and so much more that can go wrong in any individual's or family's life. These things can happen by a person's own fault, another person's fault, or nobody's fault.

History is full of bad disasters that happen on grand scales. Earthquakes in ancient china killing millions, wars have killed hundreds of millions through all history, hurricanes wiping out entire cities past and present, and the biggest of all occurring before man; the dinosaur killers and the ice ages.

Now as we can conclude, someone or something survived so life could continue. From this statement, we can conclude that life will go on no matter the disaster. This is good news; it means that after a disaster today, someone will continue life. After your disaster, your life can recover and go on.

Now I'm not talking about a solar flare or another dinosaur killing asteroid, but rather a disaster on the personal scale. If you have a disaster in your life you too will come back to life. I do not discount the possibility of your disaster lasting a while or even a life time. Some people do not get to go back home after a war, hurricane, or cancer.

I want to discus preparing for disasters in this book. My take on the whole prepper and survivalist attitude is different from the majority of survivalists and preppers who feel they have to live a life of imprisonment to some feared event that kills many people, except them because they were prepared. If you have viewed any Doomsday Preppers (DP) episode did you observe the level of fear these people live with? One guy is preparing for a solar flare, another is preparing for an asteroid to hit the earth. A third is waiting for the collapse of the US government and economy. There are even some folks out there who actually fear that real live zombies will be eating everyone soon.

Now, common sense tells us that these things don't happen, everyday. Do solar flares happen? Yes. Do asteroids hit planets? Yes. Can the US government and/or economy collapse? Yes. Can zombies eat your brains? Yes, if you are an extra in a zombie film. But really, do these things happen at such frequency that we need to worry about and fear them? No. I'll tell you what can happen any day of the week that happens to so many people every day: Job loss, injury, sickness, and death of a family member.

Each of these happens on the news or in front of you all the time. Every day, all day long, people are losing jobs, suffering a long term disability, suffering from a long term illness, and even dying unexpectedly. It happens. So get your head out of your butt and focus on the inevitable, but hopefully delayed, events of real life. Not some random end of the world disaster. The end of *your* world will happen at some point in the future.

Are you married? What if you spouse dies? Do you have parents? What if one gets cancer? Are you a hard working person? What if you get sick or injured? What if you break your back in a car wreck? What if, what if, what if? Get the point? I did.

I lost a job and could not find a good one for several years. I got sick once, and had to miss work for a month, and then I lost that one too. I got cancer and had surgery, and had to quit another. I got the point alright. If I had a prepper mentality, my life would have been easier those days. My family would have been a bit happier and less worried too.

The bigger a disaster and the more it kills or affects, the less likely it will happen. The sun going nova will kill everyone who is not on a faster than light starship. Not going to happen for billions of years. Maybe I should be worried about the sun now, and try to invent the warp engine. Nope. I will just live a life free of that worry, will you? How about a solar flare? It could take out more than half the Earth's population after a few years or more of living with the effects. Should I build a big bunker? Even though the flare might land on my bunker and still kill me because I know so much about flares that I had the foresight to build said bunker in the safe zone.

How about the United States government collapsing and its economy too? That's even more likely, and it affects less people too. I can prepare for that to some degree, even predict it more accurately than novas and flares. Now, how about worrying about a Force 5 hurricane hitting the coastal city you live in? The path is predictable. Only a few million people are affected in total. Hurricanes do happen frequently. So, maybe I should prepare for it. Ok, I can go with that in all fairness. Moving on, a five mile wide tornado takes out half a town in The Show Me State. Oh, that did happen! Hmmm. Somebody in town had a tornado shelter, and it kept them alive. Tornados happen hundreds of times a year, and affect thousands. They are just as likely to affect as little as a few cows and squirrels in the middle of Podunkville, TX.

Let's say you got in a car wreck and it was your fault. That happens to half the people involved in wrecks. Since it was your fault, the other party sues you and your insurance. You also broke your back and cannot work at your cash cow job any more. That's bad. Now you are bankrupt, unemployed, and can't feed your family.

So as we see from this discussion, the bigger the disaster, the more people affected, the less likely it will occur. On the other hand, the smaller the disaster, the fewer people affected, the more likely it will occur. A car wreck is a small disaster happening to you and maybe a few other people. They happen very, very frequently. You are affected, but your neighbors aren't. Their lives go on, but yours just ended. Sure they feel sorry for you and give you flowers, maybe even a more practical gift like donate money for some pain killers, but really they are just as happy as ever.

The end of the world happens to someone every minute of each day; maybe even every second of each day. To them it's still the end of the world. I do not write this to get you to become afraid of something bad happening to you. Rather, I want to open your eyes to a different perspective of reality.

There is something you can do for yourself, your family, maybe even for your neighbors and community. It is something that no government can do better than you can. You know what you need when you need it. You have the ability to determine your needs better than anyone else; after all, you are the one standing in the middle of any disaster seeing what you need on the spot.

If you have the fortitude to accept this reality, and the attitude to believe me about you being able to do something about this reality, then keep on reading in chapter two. If not, kiss your life good-bye. You can worry about the lack of warp drives, or deny you could get in a car wreck and I'll be no worse off for your ignorance. Your neighbors who will see you suffering, yet they have the common sense to make a step toward self-reliance, and see that you did not before the storm, might be able to help you, but then again, they might not.

By this point you may be saying to yourself, "Ok, I agree that these types of disasters can really affect my family's security, wellbeing, and comfort; but what do I do? There is so much to do to prepare. It takes lots of money to be ready to weather six months of no income."

The first thing anyone who is newly aware of the real threats to their lifestyle come to realize is how little they know about preparedness, and how much there can be to do; especially in the long run. Preparedness becomes a lifestyle that is, in a way, a lifelong journey. This is where many people panic. This is usually when the real fear comes into play. This is the point at which they think they have to do it all right now, because the disaster will happen tomorrow. This is when they adopt that one thing that they fear will happen, and become obsessive about being invulnerable to it. They wake up every day expecting it to happen. Then, they check out from reality and run away from society to the safe place because they see events happening that are not really happening.

You might agree by now you need to do something. You might even be thinking, "What do I do? I have to do it all now before it is too late!" AHHHHHHHHH!

No, you don't have to do it all now. Stop and take a breather, relax for a few moments. Take a deep breath and realize you are ok right now. Just like going on a road trip and getting lost, as long as you pull off to the side, then you can realize that you can do something very simple to eventually get back on the way. You back track a bit, go ask for directions, and get going again. The problem comes when you panic, and argue about the fact that you are lost and whose fault it is. What good does that do?

None, but you realize that even though you are lost, you will need to make a first decision, and follow through on it. You then make a second, then a third decision, taking it step by step until you are back on the way.

Prepping is the same. After you have the typical emotional panic and confusion at the first realization that things can go wrong for you and your family, you need to make a simple first step. That first simple step will give you a feeling of accomplishment. With that feeling you are ready and confident to be able to make a second, then a third. All the while you are building your confidence score and finding that things are not so overwhelming or scary.

We are not discussing these disasters so you can be afraid of them, but rather to empower you and slowly build your confidence. In the coming chapters we will discuss: how easy prepping can be; some things you can do right away to ease your immediate fear; the five most important needs we must meet in order to survive each day and related prepping strategies for each need; financial concerns related to prepping; medical and sanitary related topics; topics concerning fear; thoughts on bunkers; and strategies related to specific-disaster planning.

Hey, this isn't so hard

There are some disasters you can do a lot to be prepared for such as: medical misfortunes, loss of spouses or other family members, loss of a job, car wrecks, tornadoes, hurricanes, and other disasters that affect lesser numbers of people, but happen all the darn time.

I submit this paraphrased statement from Jack Spirko of The Survival Podcast; If you are prepared to survive a personal disaster of sorts, then you are close to being ready for many of the end of the world as we know it type of events. What does that mean? Well, when a personal disaster strikes, you still need food, water, shelter, electricity, and security of some degree or another. Just because you lose a job doesn't mean you don't eat food anymore. Surviving a tornado does not mean you never really needed a house.

Obviously, a person who calls themselves a 'survivalist' has one purpose in life, to survive until the next morning; then again the next morning, and so on. The DP survivalists store up guns, food, water, and medical kits. Well, after a disaster of some sort, one might legitimately need one or all of these. If you lose your job, have to sell the nice house and move into a bad neighborhood, your shotgun becomes more important to your feeling of security. Having a good supply of buckshot on hand will make you feel even more secure. But their lives actually look like they suck. I do not want to live like they do.

Those people look miserable, worried, and will more likely die of stress induced heart disease. They worry to such a degree that they cannot function in normal social interactions. These people usually need clozapine and other meds but do not get treated. We on the other hand do not need these drugs because we do not dream up black helicopters and chemtrails. We are just concerned that a bad time will hit and we want to live through it as comfortably as we can. We want to be able to not worry so much about bills and food. We want to be able to be the family down the street that has water when a water main breaks, or has some food when a blizzard closes the city down.

Our goal is not to live through some apocalypse, but rather just live everyday normally, even when bad times come: a life with less worry. Even if the power is out for a month, we preppers expect to live life normally as best we can. That means we are doing things and buying things that will enable us to live that close to 'normal' life.

Imagine not having to worry so much about going to the grocery store for every food need. If you had some food on hand, the burden of grocery costs will be that much lessened. Even a storage bin under the bed full of all sorts of bandages, ointments, and other items will make life a bit less worrisome.

Those of us who get the first inkling to start prepping for disasters get overwhelmed with all the things to prep for. We get blasted with lists of things to buy. As we get more into prepping, our list grows and grows, usually with items that become more and more costly. Man this is just too much, for anyone. Then we see on DP the hydroponics garden they set up for raising veggies. That can cost upwards of 5,000 bucks for that alone. Ok, I see they have their own personal armory with a hundred different rifles and pistols, not to mention all the tactical gear for ten people. Darn, that's another 40,000 bucks I've got to spend. Oh, let's not forget the five years of expensive freeze dried foods and the generators with the 2,000 gallon fuel tank buried out back.

Most important of all, now I've got to buy an underground bunker fully furnished for our comfort. I have to do what the guys on DP are doing if I'm going to survive TEOTWAWKI. Sure, if you want all your money to go into this and it be your family hobby. Ok, maybe you are a millionaire, and have nothing else better to buy, I would too. But I'm not a millionaire, and neither are you. I would like to be. Boy do I have a list of prepping supplies and stuff if I could fill my dream prepping compound with. We all have ideas for the dream, whatever it is.

Let's talk reality instead. I have limited funds, and so do you. If you are in the midst of your disaster, you really might have very limited funds, so don't even dream yet. It will cause you to lose focus on the goal of surviving, and create more stress and worry, thus destroying your mental stability. I want you to live and succeed past this disaster. Not give up. Even you too can do some things to make matters less wearisome in your disaster. One thing I wish to make clear, this is not a book about how to get through the disaster you might currently be in. You can learn and implement some of these things right in your disaster, but not much. This is for before any such event.

I want you to come to the conclusion- by way of my presentation here- that you do not need to copy cat the DP people. You can start small and cheap just as I did. I'll begin getting into the specifics of what I did, am doing, and will do, in the next chapter. In this chapter we want to feel good about our own level of participation, by way of some things that I did first, that were small and easy.

Participate to the extent that you can. Do what you can, and do it your way. To do everything in this book as it is described is not the standard of how to prepare for a disaster. In fact, I adopted many of the plans and ideas advocated by others. My introduction to prepping came by way of a newspaper interview of Jack Spirko. He is my primary source of prepping education.

I parrot Jack's stance, 'prep your way, not mine.' I provide much the same ideas as he provides. He is my inspiration for prepping. His positive attitudes lead me to believe prepping can be done sensibly. Everything I do for my own prepping, pretty much comes from him. He learned these prepping strategies from somewhere else and evolved them into so much more. He is really superb at researching, and formatting the information he learns and sharing it in an effective manner unlike any other group of survivalist advocates. After listening to his podcasts and applying his knowledge, I am now so excited by my success that I want to help proclaim his message to the world too. There is nothing more effective at spreading a message than a convert.

You do not need to buy, buy, and buy. In fact for a lot you need only devote your own sweat, for the big things. Do what you do anyway. Living life on a daily basis is a form of surviving isn't it? Do you buy a small supply of food for consumption every so often? Sure, I went shopping once a week, and then moved it to every other week because I got tired of going so often. That meant I bought more at a time, but less frequently. Most foods can stay fresh that long.

What that ended up doing was increasing my food survivability by an additional week. If the world ended, I could survive for two weeks rather than one. Hey, now I can handle it if a grocery store misses a delivery or two because of a blizzard or flood. I wasn't done yet though.

Later I realized I still hated to go every other week. So I extended my shopping to once a month, and later again to every other month. Now of course, some items I still have to shop for in between, but mostly for fresh fruits and veggies. I have faster shopping those days, and on my big trip I plan for a big segment of that day to be devoted to unloading, storing, and prepping some meal basics. I now rather enjoy my less frequent trips because I have time enough to listen to the podcast of my favorite prepping man while shopping, driving, and unloading. So I shop and learn.

I've got to give a plug to Costco. What an awesome store to shop for almost all your needs in. You can buy in bulk, and save a bit of cash. At Costco, you can buy in bulk to have a bulk supply of something. I shop there once every other month too.

Now how easy is that? As long as I plan a budget to buy that big load of food, I can handle it fine. Honestly, I have a credit card for groceries, and as long as I know I can pay it off that month, then I use it and not worry about the cash or check. Now, I am very self-disciplined in regard to credit cards because credit cards are evil. Well, not really, it's the companies who are evil. And then there are the individual suckers who screw themselves by thinking credit cards are free money machines, but that's a different book.

You don't have to do it my way, a dedicated envelope into which you contribute your weekly grocery allowance will still work. It's just fatter. Still be careful not to shop impulsively, or on an empty stomach. I'd hate to see you get yourself into trouble that way.

Now my own grocery shopping technique isn't for everyone. That's ok, if you do it your own way. My purpose behind describing it is to show you how easy it is to have a nice supply of food on hand in case of some disaster. My actual shopping technique sets me up to have food for two months and not starve if the swine flu breaks out and nobody works for the two months it is on the rampage. Grocery store workers will not be working, they are in the public. If anyone gets sick first it will be them. I'm not worried about the swine flu; Swine flu my buns, I'm concerned about my shopping in bulk to save money and time.

Let's do some easy math. Grocery shop every other month plus buy cheaply in bulk much of it, plus time saved for better things, plus food on hand for two months. Now this all adds up to…. I have prepped for some emergency and have lots of food for me and my family/friends and maybe my neighbors. In the event of some extended weather or other freak event that keeps grocery trucks from delivering, I have food.

Hey, this isn't so hard.

I hear someone out there claiming the trucks don't miss their deliveries, really? Did New York have deliveries during and after Hurricane Sandy? Do any communities receive timely deliveries before, during, and after any hurricanes? How about earthquakes? If a highway is ripped open or covered in debris, a truck can't make the delivery. Floods take time to drain away, assuming your home is not flooded or washed away. You still need to eat. Again I ask, get the point?

Now someone might legitimately ask "Why store food if it will get blown, washed, or buried to the point of not being usable?" I say, go ahead and not have food then dummy. Just because it might get buried in a quake, is not a reason to not have any. Can anyone predict the survivability of their house or not?

If having food on hand might save your life, then it is worth it. Even if in mainstream society it is considered weird to think ahead about disasters. Food on hand might make you some friends too. You can't survive alone; being able to give a box of crackers to the old lady down the block, might help her to decide to knit a scarf for you during the next blizzard and electricity is out for a month, like in Sandy.

Prepping is not a behavior, or mental issue. It is an attitude, and a lifestyle. Think back to our American forefathers. They did not have refrigerators, freezers, grocery stores, or plumbing. Nor did they have electricity to help them stay warm or cool. Obviously they survived and thrived, or we wouldn't be here. The 1600's era colonist had it rough compared to today, but they didn't know it. They just did what they did every day. Eat, work, and sleep.

Hey, we do that too. They stored up from the harvest from their own gardens and fields. Actually nearly everybody had a garden or field to grow their own food in. Then they did stuff to keep the food through winter when plants don't grow. They kept all sorts of food stored in many different ways. Months and months of food kept on hand.

They had so much food on hand that the community got together and shared a big harvest feast, the predecessor to Thanksgiving. This was everyday living for those folks: Canning, pickling, and drying. Prepping is a beneficial lifestyle, not a mental issue.

The most important prep

As mentioned before, the most common of disasters are those that are small enough to affect only individuals or families. As I wrote this book, a wonderful family in my town was devastated by a rock slide. This rock slide did not destroy their home, but rather them. They were on a day hike; mom, dad, big sister, little sister, and two cousins. They went to enjoy a hike and picnic on a commonly traveled hiking trail to a pretty waterfall.

It was a beautiful day, I remember because I was working with a young Down Syndrome boy when I heard the local search and rescue teams driving off with their sirens on We were throwing a football during a break.

It had been raining frequently for several weeks prior to the hike. The trail they took is under cliffs that often shed large segments due to rainfall. The weather also began to have new lows during the night that would hit freezing. With moisture in the cliff materials and freezing temps, frost action began to affect the structure of the cliff faces.

By shear chance this family chose to hike on the day that a big release occurred. There was only one survivor, a 13 year old girl that I knew because I got to be her substitute teacher a few times. Her world has ended for the next several years.

There was not an asteroid ending her world. There was no CME or anything else that we normally think of that would end the world; just a bunch of rocks on a mountainside.

Why do I bring up this example? Because one thing that occupied my mind after it was how she would be for the next few years until she became an adult. Who will take care of her? Who will look out for her financial interests? Did her parents have wills? Did they have insurances for themselves and the other daughter? If so who will make sure she gets these things.

These are not things people think of right after such a disaster, but after a while they are things that will come up. Will they become a nightmare? Will she have to relive the feelings and loneliness that fighting a probate court or other family members will bring back to life?

Too many people who do not want to think about such trouble will take the irresponsible path by saying "I'll be dead, I don't care." They do not care what trouble their loved one will have to go through to retain their rights to family property and insurance. What if it was a matter of their survivor(s) living in poverty or comfort? Would they care then?

I most certainly would care. Very much so. I would like to think that you might too. I cannot make you care, but maybe if you are tempted to feel like not caring, I could ease you into doing so. Pretend you have a 13 year old daughter. Pretend you and your spouse die in some freak accident. Do you have the paperwork in place for her to be adopted by the family member or other people that you trust to love them and raise them into adulthood and beyond?

Or would you rather not care, and gamble that the foster system will have their best interests at heart. Add your insurance policies to this mess. If you are not prepared in this regard, maybe the bad brother who has been in jail will be the one who takes her in because he can benefit from the million dollar policy.

I am just thinking of the worst case. Who knows what could happen? Take time today to get this in order. The family I discussed did not expect to die in a rock slide on a beautiful day. The family on the news you heard about did not expect to lose someone in a boating accident or during a church retreat.

If you would like for your death to be one that will not haunt and harass them for an extended period, then make the process go as smoothly as can be possible. Get you wills worked out. Get your living will worked out too, so that survivors do not have conflicts that last a lifetime. Take the time to plan for the care that your children will need tomorrow, today. I am telling you that many children lose their parents everyday in car crashes and other unexpected events. So might yours.

Be sure that all insurances are up to date in how you want them distributed. Plan for the future as related to the possibility of your death, your spouse's death, or even both of your deaths.

Another possible point of struggle for survivors is who will be the Medical Power Of Attorney for you. Get this done so that you can choose who will execute any decisions that might need to be decided. Get these things done now because you love your survivors and do not want them to go through hell getting you taken care of. Prevent conflict over paying bills and accessing money in banks and other places. Prevent any temptation to take advantage of money in your accounts or stocks.

When you die, the government will still want your taxes. Who will be responsible for this? Who will be saddled with debt if you owe sizable amounts? All of these topics are not what people want to talk about when they discuss surviving the big event. It is not macho to think about debt and taxes. It is not fun to think about your survivors fighting each other for the rest of their lives over one of them pulling the plug.

Do you want your family to go through such hardships?

Do not throw these things to the wind and let them fall how they might. We are discussing those you love. We are discussing the amount of money and time they will have to spend to protect what you might leave them.

The next chapter focuses on what a new prepper can do now. These are methods discussed by Jack that he found to be the most effective and fastest means of gaining a rudimentary level of preparedness. I use some of them and found that they put me in the position to face the many disasters which do occur somewhere everyday. I want you to have the same feelings of security that I gained when I did them. These will only provide you with the basic means of surviving your typical shorter term disasters such as big storms. They are not meant to keep you alive after a solar flare.

Following this, each of the next five chapters will be on one of the five basic requirements of survival and preparation, describing what it is and why it is. They are in no particular order of importance because each is important at the time it is needed. The five needs of a person to survive are: Food, water, security, shelter, and energy.

Like I said, they are not in any order of importance. Yeah, water is needed daily, but a gun will keep you alive, maybe, when it is needed. One might live longer because they had a means of security. A bullet can kill faster than thirst. Even the cold can kill faster than thirst. So no one is more important than the others when it comes to the exact time they are in need of being fulfilled.

What to do now to feel ready

As discussed in chapter 1, we talked about how the new prepper can suddenly feel overwhelmed about what to do. This chapter is the discussion in which I relay to you what you can do now to provide for each of the most important needs, to live through a disaster or event.

These things will cost some money, but not much as the more advanced prepper strategies discussed in the later chapters. Some are free and only require a change in habits and frame of mind. The most costly will be the food, and the power solution. These things are lifestyle strategies that are similar to those that our grandparents did within their technological ability, especially food and fuel. These are things that any responsible adult should do anyway, so as not to be so dependent on the government rescuing us from our own passivity.

So what is the first thing a beginning prepper should do to have a supply of food on hand? Go buy double or triple what you normally do or a crate of MREs? Not exactly, most people new to this think, "What if I have to go several months without the ability to buy from a store because of the dreaded bad events everyone fears?" I can tell you a fast and cheap way to get some food on hand that will store well for many years that I learned from Jack Spirko; he sure is a really practical and productive man. This is a method that is done only to help a new prepper beat the immediate panic. It is a fire and forget method that will enable a family to have some food on hand for nearly any imaginable emergency.

Go buy three food grade tubs that can be sealed air tight; fill each with the basics; beans, rice, and pastas from the grocery store; buy a pack of hand warmers and put one hand warmer in each tub; close them and store them in a cool and dry place like a closet or basement. Buy a case of freeze dried meats and store it too. You can do the buckets for under a hundred bucks, and the freeze dried stuff for another few hundred.

Double the amount if your family is larger. This gives you calories and protein that can be stuck aside and only there for the event that you have no other food sources in any given circumstance. This food stored this way will stay edible longer than you will probably live. Its taste might not be the best but if needed it will keep you alive. There, now you are ready to eat when others could be starving. This is only to help you feel secure and to place you in a feeling that will enable you to move forward into more advanced food storage prepping methods, if you so choose.

Do not go out and buy so much that you can fill your basement. I am only discussing an amount that can be stored in a closet on the floor, back out of the way. This is only enough to last a few weeks or so. This is enough to get you through a hurricane, blizzard or whatever, and the period of time it might take for the official help to arrive.

For the purposes of getting an immediate store of water for any emergency during which water becomes unavailable; save about 50 two-liter pop bottles and/or one gallon Arizona tea jugs. These particular jugs can be gathered free from neighbors, or what you might buy anyway when you buy soda and tea. Both styles of bottles are made of food quality plastic that is very acid resistant, and can handle rougher handling. I've dropped full two liters from 6 feet up and they don't explode or crack so easily. The tea jugs are not as durable in regards to dropping, but they are quite thick. The 2 liters can stack easily enough to store many of them in a sideways position as long as there are end caps to keep them from rolling.

Clean them real good, then fill and forget them in a dark place; under beds, in closets, in the basement or crawlspace, or if your climate allows for it, outdoors in a shed or shelter. Darkness prevents algae growth inside the bottles. Leave enough space in each for expansion if they will be frozen. A single drop of chlorine bleach will also help preserve the water for very long term storage, but it is not really needed. You can get into the habit of rotating these later if you so desire to keep the flavor of water fresher, but that is not that important at this stage.

This is the cheapest way to store water. It is essentially free, especially if you mooch the bottles from neighbors and fill from the faucet. It would be costly at 10 bucks a jug to buy 20 of the 5 gallon jugs to keep under the house. It is also rather costly to go buy the single serve cases of bottled water at the stores. Five bucks per 24-pack will add up quickly. I am not saying to not buy maybe a few though. Use them as you normally do if you already are in the habit of buying cases. Buy and store extras, then rotate them in normal use. This works for those who already buy 5 gallon jugs too. I only offer you a cheaper route. What an easy way to store water. This too is a storage method I learned from Jack. He sure is good at seeing the most practical way of doing things.

Buy a cheap filter set up for emergency use too.

Now as I said, you are ready to face a few days without water. Combine these options to extend your supply. This is a most appropriate strategy for urban dwellers that rely on the city services. Now, when you feel safe and calm enough that you are no longer feeling the panic of supplying your hydration needs, you are ready to move on to more advanced water related prepping methods.

Unless you are one of the destitute on the streets or living out of your car; you have shelter. I don't care if it is where you wish to live or not. For the purpose of immediate preparation, you have shelter. However, you need to keep in mind what to do for shelter if your current location is so heavily damaged that you cannot remain. You need to plan this out now. Where will you go? Do you have family within an hour drive or two? Can you afford an extended stay in a hotel or similar place? Discuss this with anyone who might be able to provide a temporary place to stay.

The next basic need is energy, and if you live anywhere already, then you have plenty to meet any needs. Again, if your shelter is lost, then you lose electricity for a time. This is most easily provided by relocating as discussed above.

But, if you do not lose your shelter, just its power, this can be solved for with yet another immediate solution as discussed by Jack. Many of us get our power from the grid, and we all know what to have in the event it goes down for a few days... a generator and fuel. Fortunately, we all have a generator; our cars. Also, we are very dependent on fuel for transport.

Go buy six to twelve yellow or red five gallon fuel containers (depending on the fuel your generator and/or most used vehicle require.) Once a month, for the next six to twelve months, go fill up a single five gallon container with the fuel of choice. Number or label them monthly as you fill them. This is not much extra money for your monthly fuel bill. When you run out of containers, once a month, take the first one, and dump it in your vehicle's tank. Go refill it when you fill your car and move it to the back of the line. Repeat this each month from now on. You'll be rotating it at a frequency such that you will not allow the fuel to degrade, because you will add a fuel preservative to each container. Now you will have sixty gallons of fuel ready to use if needed, and used monthly anyway.

This gives you the flexibility to have an immediate supply of fuel built up for transport or power production in a generator. You may not live in a place that will allow for fuel storage, like an apartment. Go get a cheap storage place for 30 bucks a month and store it there. If you can get a climate controlled one, then you can store some food, water, and other things there. This way it is not at your residence when your shelter might be damaged.

Think about how much better the experiences of Sandy and Katrina victims would have been if they had a few containers of fuel on hand or easily accessible. Some did, you can hear the story of their successful lives on Jack's podcast. Think about how simple an idea of using your car as a generator is.

Ok, the generator you already own is in your car. This is another strategy advocated by Jack, that he got from a man named Steven Harris. Your vehicle's engine is not any different than a generator you can buy at Lowes. Well, one difference, it produces twelve volts rather than 120. This can be fixed by the purchase of an auto inverter on Amazon. These guys recommend a 400 to 1000 watt unit. You will connect this directly to your vehicle's battery, not the power socket.

You will need to buy a few heavy duty extension cords and splitters. Connect them to the inverter and run them in to your garage then into your house. Do not run the vehicle in the garage. You do not need to run the engine continually, just run it for your freezer and fridge for 30 minutes to an hour every so often. You can now run nearly any appliance or item for your convenience.

You will also need to buy and keep on hand an extra change of oil for the vehicle. Possibly sparkplugs. You also will need to buy small cords of LED lights for use to light up the residence. Keep all the cords, spares, and lights in a big tub that can be easily reached when needed. Keep a few headlamps, flashlights, radios, phone chargers, and rechargeable batteries and charger handy in strategic places about the house. You will also need a smart charger for cars. You now have a temporary generator solution and fuel solution for any immediate need for such.

The next basic need to meet is security. Keep this simple, make sure all the latches and locks about the house are in full working condition; if they are not then fix/replace them. Keep your home and vehicles properly locked and things of value out of sight. Most thefts occur because doors are open or unlocked. Be aware of security risks, such as family names on the back of your car and exposure on social websites. Be aware of your surroundings at all times. Where do you visit an ATM, or fill your gas tank? Take measures to keep you and your family safe when doing your daily habits.

When you need security, you need it then and there. Effective law enforcement is a factor, but there have been times when it was not effective. Besides, even effective law enforcement cannot stop you from doing something stupid that increases your odds of being victimized. Laws that regulate us from leaving keys in the ignition do not prevent auto theft if you still leave the keys in it. Be aware of your actions and learn the related actions that will help you not be victimized.

With all this in mind, you still might be victimized regardless of how vigilant you are about your behavior patterns. You need the means to hinder a crime in your own home and cars. Things to help in these locations are discussed later, but for now what can you get to add to the security of your castles?

Non-lethal defense tools such as pepper spray are very inexpensive compared to guns. Plus they are family friendly in that if a kid gets it in their hands, they find life unpleasant for a few hours, but they get to live. Buy some redundancy in these types of items and keep them about the home and car in hidden but accessible locations. Train yourself as to the locations of each item so when they are needed, you will act instinctively when they are needed.

Maybe you already have this, but a common and effective addition to home security is the ownership of a dog. You are trading a bed and food for the instinctive territorial sense that dogs of all sizes have. Criminals will avoid anything that will direct attention to where they are perpetrating, or where they might get perforated.

These strategies discussed in this chapter have been included for one purpose; to give ideas that anyone can do that will provide for an immediate solution to meeting survival needs in almost any common small scale disaster event. They can be stand alone actions for those who do not wish to go any deeper into the preparedness lifestyle, but they can be stepping stones to more effective and long term solutions to one's potential obstacles during any longer term events. These will make you flexible to many of life's standard knock down moments.

Read on for more ideas and strategies to make you more self-reliant and resilient in hardship.

Get the basics first: Food

As I said, I will discuss the why's and how's of each requirement's being a requirement. Food: Got to have it. There, that's why it is on the list. Yeah, maybe I can go a week without eating, but I sure in heck won't have the ability to chase a rabbit after a week of starving. I will end up laying on the ground whining for the rest of the theoretical month it takes to starve to death.

I can go a day comfortably; some can't do that and handle it mentally. Some cannot go a few hours without due to medical problems. But by the time a week comes around, I'm really down for the count. So my ideal food requirement to survive any event is to not go more than a day or two without eating. I can ration my food to make it last a good time longer that way, but I will lose weight and look more scraggly than my 150 lbs does now when well fed. Ideally, I want to eat every day.

So do you, I'm sure. That's why I chose food to be first. I already talked some about food and prepping in the previous chapter. I described a way of changing a habit to adjust for having more food on hand longer, except that last week before shopping.

Why should we have extra food on hand anyway? As discussed earlier, if a blizzard shut the roads down, how does food make it to the store? We all have seen the grocery stores emptied of their three day inventory before a one day ice storm. Some of you may have seen the stores go empty before a local hurricane hit your region. At the least, we have all seen this discussed on the news. By the way, food is not the only thing flying off the shelves in times of panic buying by uninformed sheeple.

If the trucks can't make it, and you are one of those daily shoppers who is in the store every single day; what ya going to eat? I remember hearing about some riots in London years back.

The grocery stores there could not get food for a week. London, riots? It could happen in Atlanta, where some welfare recipients went nuts because the food stamp cards were delayed one day from being refilled due to a technical glitch. What would happen if they couldn't refill for a week, or a month? Man that sounds scary for Atlanta's residents in the areas near ghettoville.

It could happen in any American city with high concentrations of mad, entitled people who think they deserve welfare food stamps. "Where's my welfare?" a lady cried on the news camera. Notice she said "my" as though she can't grasp the concept that tax payers are donating money (involuntarily) to her. Yeah, there are many good folks getting legitimately deserved assistance, but they don't claim it is theirs like we claim our car is ours.

If you live in a city like the above, you better have food on hand if the riots shut down the city. That of course is not the only reason to have extra food on hand. Another reason to have food on hand is if you lose a job or suffer an injury, or whatever else might cause you to not have the good income that you and your family have come to rely on. Maybe a big supply of groceries on hand will make you not worry about the need to spend money during the immediate term. However, the longer the financial crisis occurs, the more of a need to have money to buy groceries will occur.

In addition to his emergency food setup I described in chapter 3. Many people in the prepping community recommend that everyone should have a minimum of 30 days of food on hand. This can be done easily by the method I discussed in Ch. 2. Go shopping less often, and buy more. Buy in bulk enough to last a month or two. All dry goods will last that long and way longer anyway. Frozen products last quit a while too, if kept in a freezer that does not have a frost free cycle. That's why foods get freezer burn. Their surfaces thaw out and are quickly refrozen over and over again. Buying dry goods and frozen goods will allow us to hold on to many foods longer than a week at a time. Buying like this will get you through the time period most disasters take to clear up. In fact, one could easily have and continually use a supply of six months to a year of food through grocery shopping habits and proper rotation of the food.

Grocery shopping can only do so much towards having a substantial supply of food on hand. For the longer term events, like losing a house to a flood, having food in one spot doesn't help any. If the house is a loss, then the food will be too. For the beginner, this is a problem. Preppers advocate for us to have a location to go to if we have to leave. Evacuate when it is recommended, and you can take a great supply of food and stuff with you. Having a second place is costly and a big commitment.

This is where I say, if you can't do a second place, yeah, you're vulnerable, but it's not too likely to happen. Instead, maybe you have a family member or a good friend on the other side of town, or within a couple of hours drive from your home. Work out a deal for you to make this your bug out location for a week or longer. Stage items there too. The best thing would be if they read this book too and were motivated to do a little prepping with you. Agree to make each other the other's bug out location.

As mentioned earlier, an additional reason to have an even longer lasting store of food on hand is the loss of a job or some other long term event that prevents your family from receiving an adequate income. Groceries are expensive, and that will not change, except to continue increasing due to inflation created by this nation's monetary policies through the Federal Reserve System.

Let's say that you have a six month store of food on hand, not necessarily MREs or freeze dried camping/survival foods, but groceries that you buy already. What that could mean is that it might be six months before you have to spend what little money you have on groceries. Maybe you decide to make lunches and dinners only from that store of food, and then you will only be buying breakfast foods and save 2/3rds of the grocery money. You could even make one meal a day and save that much money too. However you do it is up to you, but any meals not bought means money saved and less worry financially.

How do you get that much food on hand by only grocery shopping, not other food storage methods? First you need to keep an ongoing list of foods you eat each day for a month or two. Observe what it is you buy, and then go copy can. Copy canning is a shopping strategy that involves you buying double (or more) of what you plan on buying already. Let's say last month you used four cans of green beans. You always buy that many beans in any given month. Well next time, buy eight cans of green beans. Now you have two months of green beans available.

The only problem, that can be easily solved, is where do I store that much food, and how do I make sure it does not go bad? If you really do use the four cans every month, then just keep using them normally, but stack your cans in such a way that as you buy new cans, you are putting those newest purchases in the back and rotating your food. Just like grocery stores should be doing. They stock the freshest can of product in the rear of the shelf and pull forward the ones that have been on the shelf the longest.

You can store food in unique places, like in a closet. Yeah, I know many of us have limited space, but find a way that will work for you. As I said, you could easily store six months worth, or even up to a year's worth of some foods this way. Make sure you are doing this with foods you really do eat on a frequent basis. Also, make certain you are not buying foods you don't like to eat. In any of the bad situations we've discussed, it will be an even worse situation because you are not eating enjoyable, familiar foods. I want to survive in as much comfort as is possible, don't you?

Some foods you cannot do this style of shopping and storing with. Fresh veggies and fruits do not store long at all. If you do lose an income for a long time, at least you could have a long period of food resilience and lower grocery costs. If you only have to go buy fresh foods when you need them, then you are still saving money.

The lesson here is to learn how to have plenty of food on hand, not because of the end of the world, but because your world might end for a year or two. Life will go on, you will find a new job, if not as good, but at least it will help.

Some survivalist's do store several years' worth of food. They do this by using additional strategies: such as canning, freeze drying, MREs, and more. This may or may not be useful to you. If you are not interested in this, that is ok. With the grocery store only method, you are now ready to survive nearly all bad disasters, such as a year of depression style economic events. I consider you to be prepared in relation to food storage.

If you seek more food storage or even some variety, then add some long term food storage products to your storage plans. Many companies produce food intended to store for many years in the proper storage environment. One of my favorites is Thrive. They make organic varieties of what others make. Add whatever you feel you would like for variety. I add their breakfast choices, because it is harder to find for storage. Most long term foods are lunch and dinner style food.

There is one additional way of easy food storage. It will require more time, but can be done cheaply. Depending on where you live this method can be done year round, or only during the summer. It is gardening. I live in Texas so I can garden certain plants outdoors year round, especially with greenhouses and other cold weather gardening tech. Growing your own food, using the cheapest garden bed construction you can, will save you money. If you are in a money conscious situation, gardening is a great means of not only saving money, but not having to buy the cheapest, most refined, industrial, toxic foods that poor people commonly by in America. Gardens will provide top shelf nutrition for your family, not to mention a mentally relaxing hobby to distract you from daily worries and fears. Buy twenty bucks of seeds that grow the veggies you most use and like. You will certainly get a massive amount of food from such a purchase. You will certainly make back that twenty bucks.

Please keep in mind that if you have not had any prior gardening experience, you will have disappointments. It can be hard to learn gardening, especially if you think you have to plant the big garden right away. Start small. Pick one or two veggies you like and make a small patch. Afterward, you will have built a bit more confidence in your budding skills. Expand by a small amount every year. Do not make the mistake of pressuring yourself by envisioning the grand garden that can feed your every veggie need in one season. You will fail, and then give up.

Start small... I did, or still am. I started with a bed 6x2 with lettuce, spinach, carrots, and scallions. They did ok, the next year I added an irrigation system and a second 6x2 bed for green beans and cabbage. They all did a bit better the second year. This year as I write this, my third year, I moved and built a new first bed 15x3. I trellised 10 green beans, and planted 40 carrots, 20 lettuce, 4 cabbage, 6 banana peppers, and 6 chards. This bed I built is a woody bed. I filled a foot deep hole with 3 inch branches, and filled in the dirt with lots of compost. I mulched it with 2 inches of wood shavings, and this is the best garden I've done yet.

Next, for winter I will build a row cover and plant all plants that can handle low temps. Next year, I will plant raspberries, and make a water melon patch. I will plant a few things more, if I can; but not too much more. I do not want to overload myself and fail. With this garden I am now harvesting a little as I need lettuce and such. I no longer buy lettuce, and soon it will be that way for carrots. I am still experimenting on when to plant and when to harvest. I also am learning how to keep food in the ground over the hot summers. There is a lot to learn about, but I know this, if I can gain some knowledge about growing food, I will be able to lean on it in times of need. So can you.

Don't forget all our furry and feathered friends out there; they need food too. Pet foods can be purchased, stored, and rotated just as easily as human foods. Food for livestock might be a requirement if you pasture animals in small pens and already feed them outside foods. If you have large track of land this is not a problem for many animals. Keep this in mind and plan ahead for your situation.

Keeping livestock of varied kinds can also be a means of storing food. Beef can stay fresh for years, if it is alive. This applies to others too, such as chickens, pigs, and fish. If you can keep them fed, you can keep yourself fed. Especially pastured and/or low density groupings. Livestock is more acceptable a choice in rural areas; however, some urban and suburban areas allow some small livestock. This might involve additional learning for you and me. We can have ample food in any circumstance short of the *final* disaster.

Gardening and raising livestock introduce other advanced food storage options as mentioned before; such as canning fruits, veggies, and meats; drying/dehydrating the same; and freezing the same. These are traditional and proven methods of long-term storage of foods.

My feelings concerning any disaster prepping plan needs to at least acknowledge the growing and raising your own food to improve your flexibility. I say acknowledge because not everyone has the means. Some folks live apartments and other similar circumstances that do not allow gardening or livestock. Do what you can, maybe aim for a goal of having a place for such, if you feel the need. Storage can only take you so far in a chronological sense. Eventually you will run out of food; even water. Consider these two more intensive options for the future, if not for the present.

Water: It's not just for swimming in

Most people suffer from a common mental syndrome I call the "What can go wrong today, we are so advanced" syndrome. It is common for people to think that nothing can go wrong in today's society. We have nuclear power, super duper computers that can map the universe and DNA, and even limited space travel. What can we not figure out?

How about how to stay alive longer than a few days without water? Try it and see if you can come up with some way that does not involve splicing cactus genes into our own. Although, I kind of like the idea of having the genetic information for our bodies to produce chloroplasts in our skin cells. Imagine if we could produce some of our own dietary intake by getting some sun time. That could save a lot of money in groceries.

Good idea, but it won't help us not thirst to death. We need water every day. Go without for a whole day and you notice a change in your energy levels. When I get a bit dehydrated, I get sleepy. A drink of water gets me going again. There are many situations in which we can lose our source of clean water for a short period of time. In our nation, floods compromise our safe water every year. On the news we see people in Africa dying of Cholera, a disease that occurs when someone ingests water contaminated by sewage.

It has only been about a century and a half that doctors learned about washing hands before surgery. People get cholera in the US too. Unbelievable isn't it? This nation there is not a city without water treatment plants. But, when a flood happens to backwash those plants, they pump dirty water not fit to drink. That is why our government always announces in flood ravaged areas a boiling advisory. We do it too, just to be on the safe side. They even announce one when a water main breaks. You never know, do you?

Water thus becomes an essential part of a disaster preparedness plan. In my mind there are only two options, I do them both; store water and/or filter water. Storing water can be either cheap or expensive. After following the 'do it now' storage method discussed in chapter 3, you are ready to take a step toward a more lifestyle focused preparation.

This next step is to filter water because a person can store only so much water. Filtering does require an initial investment, and an ongoing cost. Filter elements need replacement after so much use or time sitting unpackaged. They can be costly, depending on the brand and quality. The most expensive is the whole house filter and sink systems. The maintenance cost is higher too. I use a faucet adapter most because of the convenience, but it is not my only means. I have Berkey water filters that allow me to fill an upper storage portion and gravity filter into a lower storage point. They come in varied sizes and also have replaceable filters. They also require an up front purchase, and then you might like to buy the filters in bulk to keep on hand.

Why go to this trouble? As I mentioned earlier, cities can have compromised water systems. Yes, big modern, flashy, American cities and towns do have unreliable water systems. If power goes out, the pumps can no longer fill the water towers. The filtering itself will not get done either. Eventually, the faucet will go dry.

Sometimes floods will overflow into the clean water pools at treatment facilities. New Orleans really had a case of this. Salt water, sewage, chemicals, all got into the water system there. How long were people told to not use city water? I don't know at this time, but I'm confident in my guess of more than a month. Don't forget the nasty and unhealthful treatment chemicals of fluoride and chlorine. I try to minimize my intake of two elements that have been proven toxic. How long would a store of 500 gallons last for dinking and cooking? Don't forget about flushing the toilet with a bucket filled and poured into the toilet bowl. Bathing and cleaning cloths and other things might be a problem with only 500 gallons.

I am not saying we need to go get cisterns and storage tanks, unless you can. I do say have a lot of water stored somehow if at least for drinking and cooking. There are ways to help. Delay bathing for longer periods, think of a disaster as a campout, a long campout. People do it all over the world anyway in their poverty stricken lives. It can be done. Most disaster will not be so long that you have to delay bathing, but it can happen; think Katrina.

Wear cloths longer, not just for one day. The disaster will pass. I realize that some disasters leave people without homes and even jobs, but for now I am only focusing on the need and use of water for an emergency. Having even a few days of clean water on hand can make a difference between life and sickness that could result in death. This is even more important if you live in arid regions.

I once lived in the mountains in Colorado. My plan was that I would drive over to the mountain river that ran through town, fill up some large containers, and go back and filter the water in my Berkey, then boil it too. This water would have been for drinking and cooking only. I could fill a trash can this same way and use it to dip water for flushing the toilets.

Since I moved to the city, this has not been a workable solution. I am currently without stored water, but I can filter in the event of contamination of city supply. I will be more ready soon though. One can collect and store rain water, but it will need filtering and boiling too. This doesn't work so well in Phoenix like it might in Seattle. Your local climate will make a big difference. Having rather close water sources such as lakes and rivers helps greatly. Be sure to filter and boil. Traveling back and forth might not be safe or ideal.

The need for you to drink is not the only concern; pets need water too. Again, this depends on your locality. If you have natural sources, animals can drink from them. Plan accordingly to your situation. Any livestock also needs to be taken into consideration. Can you provide for a herd of cows, or even two? A possible solution to this can kill two birds with one stone. Rainwater collection can provide for human, plant, and animal use; but be sure to filter and boil according to your needs. Gardens won't need filtering and neither will livestock and pets.

You need some water storage, but will need a means of filtering outside sources of water too. I think any plan for disaster prepping should include both. Water is so important to have around. I could go into more detail by providing lots of how-to information, but one can go elsewhere for that. I only wish to provide a basic strategy that can be easily followed by folks who have many other things to think about in daily life. I want my readers to feel that they can have a plan and not be overwhelmed by the DP mentality.

There is an additional subject of great importance of water; that is sanitation. Water is a solvent at the atomic level. That is what makes it so useful in bathing and washing things. You use water to wash food and other related compounds off the dishes, to wash dirt from your hands, and to clean surgical tools. You can increase its effectiveness by warming it up and adding some soap.

Disease prevention is the most common use of water in relation to sanitation; we use it to flush away body waste, rinse rotten food down the drain, and clean a fresh cut or scrape. These everyday uses of water will become the difference between life and death in a disaster. After an initial disaster actually occurs, more people die from diseases than any other cause.

Diseases like cholera, dysentery, and other water borne illnesses, kill more people in third world countries than any other causes of death. That can't happen here in America or any other first world nation. Well it did and does. Our nation's history is replete with folks dying of these diseases. During all the settlement phases people were dying from cholera. During any wars our nation has participated in more soldiers died from sickness than from weapons.

Today, people get sick during water main breaks, and they certainly died due to the aftermath of Katrina. Mostly the very young and the old die from these things when a slight hiccup occurs in our infrastructure. Not so far back Hurricane Sandy really cause a big hiccup in the Northeast. Cities were without water and electricity for weeks.

I feel that people who live in desert regions are not the only people who will have hard times getting water during a system failure. Cities and suburban areas are deserts in a way. You might be puzzled by my thinking, but think about where water comes from in cities and suburbs. Water is piped and stored in tanks, then distributed through more pipes. The water often comes from far away; far enough away that a person could not walk with buckets to refill. Yeah some places have a river through town that the water comes from, some have nearby lakes, or even sea water sources. Some small communities have lakes, ponds, and creeks.

In these places one can walk over and collect some water; however, some of those same places might go dry real quick, especially if everyone is in need of water. Living in a suburban or urban area is not the most safe or convenient place to be spending time going back and forth for water. It might open you up to being a victim of violence because some folks would be too lazy to gather for themselves when people are doing it and can be targeted for theft.

Did you see the BBC series Survivors? How many times were any of the people in that show victimized? Keeping a store of water on hand at home in a pool is one solution. Using rain catchment is good too. One can only store so much water, but keeping enough around to get by until help arrives or the time of danger passes is a way to mitigate any risks.

You get the point? Next week the big one could hit SanFran, and the most deadly threat will be the potential for disease to break out. Clean water is the only way to prevent such occurrences. You will need some means of fresh, clean water for many uses, if municipal water is not available, no matter the cause of its loss.

This includes being able to boil it, drain it, flush waste, clean things, and drink it. Maybe you should consider a way to pressurize it, so that it can flow too. Plan you system by placing the storage at some point up gradient, or higher than the place you want it to come out at. Use gravity for free.

Security: The bad guys kill too

There are more ways to die than by thirst or starving. Death by crime is very common, but will become more so in many disaster situations. This aspect of survival is generally viewed as the point of scorn by those who view Preppers as nuts. It takes only one criminal to kill you and your family, or do much worse. Being a victim might mean not surviving. Having a means of self defense might be the difference. Crime does not happen in disasters alone, it happens daily. I again refer you to the news. Every day, it is filled with victims of crime.

Another topic in the realm of personal security is related to one's attitude about the criminal element. Many people believe that they do not need to be concerned about being victimized because nothing ever happens in our nice picket fence neighborhood of all white folks.

People cannot wrap their heads about the idea that even in the perfect neighborhood, there is always some small percentage of people who are bad. The only reason they do not act on such compulsions is that the societal consequences keep them in check. They really do not want to go to jail, but they seek other outlets to their desires. You see on the news how it is always some nice guy that commits the horrible murder. Folks never suspected that the kind person is a pedophile.

What would happen if things get bad like they did in Katrina? The rumors of rape, and the proven fact of gangs raiding homes and businesses motivated people to protect themselves. Even harder to believe is that the N.O. police went around confiscating peoples personal firearms in total disregard for the 2nd Amendment. Sure, when times are normal and there are not events that cause the average person to fear for their needs, there will not be a threat to most people's safety. When something bad does happen it is just a statistic that involved someone else; never us.

But can you be certain that will not change under other circumstances. There have been times when events bring out the normal in some people and bring out the worst in others. By normal I mean the bad people. Once they see an opportunity to do what their evil hearts crave, they will. They will go rape someone simply because they know they can get away with it. We know they will go rob a store, by smashing the windows when they see the chance. They do it in riots and panics. They do it during evacuations like during Katrina. Honestly, we expect bad guys to act this way when given the chance.

Even more disturbing though is the idea of our friendly neighbor snapping during a time of hardship. They may be starving and they cannot stand to see their kids suffering. They begin to get angry because they cannot get the food as easily as before. Maybe it costs too much for whatever reason. Eventually they become more desperate, and they make a choice to go get what they can, however they can, because they need something for the family. They see you leave your home, and they know you have stuff they need. Maybe they get to the point that they do not even wait for you to leave. They feel so entitled that you have to share, that they come straight to you and try taking it by force.

Can any of us honestly say that even we do not begin to think similarly? I hope not, but such a temptation can be completely avoided by being prepared in regards to food and water. You cannot totally be certain how you would act in times of utter starvation; can you predict what someone else may do in such times?

Being armed is the most common form of self defense. There is such controversy over guns in particular, but you might be victimized with a knife, axe, bread roller, brick, bat, crowbar, or whatever the criminal mind can come up with. Gun laws do not keep crime from happening. In China, the strictest nation concerning guns in my opinion, it is becoming more common to hear about knife wielding nutters killing school kids. Even the total absence of guns does not prevent mass murders. By the way, the FBI releases crime stats every year, and more people die by knives than by guns. Think about it and be ready for the disaster of a mugging or home invasion. The police will be too late most of the time, and you or a loved one might just be dead if you cannot defend yourself and them.

There is one reason the gun is called 'the great equalizer.' You become equal with the bad guys. They will think twice about committing a crime against an armed person. It has been proven to be the case. Surveys of inmates reveal that the inmates generally avoided homes and businesses known to have armed residents and owners.

Having food and water is all good, and important. But the moment you need to defend yourself, it will not help. It may even be the reason they are seeking to victimize you. You will need to defend your stores from the small percent of evil people out there that come out of the cracks during disasters. If they know you have food and water, they will come for it. This is a small part of society, but they do exist, be ready.

Defense can be argued to be the most important of the needs; this argument is supported by the daily operations of any combat unit. Before they eat, or settle down, they do their security procedures; a resting unit will first 'dig in' before resting. Security is paramount.

Surely you realize I am not discussing this in relation to a job loss or injury. Other than being ready for the everyday possibility to protect your family and friends; any of the bigger disasters will bring out the worse in some people who were nice and honest before. Defense is paramount for you at such times. In this I repeat what was discussed in chapter 3, change your situational awareness. This is the first step to being secure.

Beyond the initial security changes related to situational awareness, my solution is to buy a gun. You might eventually decide to buy more than one. My recommendation is to start with a shotgun. Not some tactical shotgun, but a hunting shotgun. I learned from my favorite survival podcasting guy a common sense reason to this. Unfortunately, in today's world, politicos run the American justice system. Some run it in such a way that prevents people from protecting themselves. They even go so far to punish folks who do protect themselves. I can imagine a prosecutor who shows the jury your tactical awesome and aggressive looking shotgun and says, "There is only one reason to have a gun that looks like this. That is to kill. This person wanted to kill from the beginning."

That could be you defending yourself from such a gun hating prosecutor. Avoid the hype from the survival paranoids who say to buy a Main Battle Rifle (MBR). You don't need one. I was once asked by one what my favorite MBR was. I didn't answer because it doesn't matter. A good hunting shotgun will work well enough. I do not reasonably expect to be fighting aliens in the streets. Could happen, if we're not alone, but I doubt it. I own a Mossberg Turkey Thug. It has camouflage colored plastic to look like a hunting gun. It even is named as a hunting gun. It looks like a tactical pump, but its name says otherwise. Of course you can always get the standard long barrel shotgun too. Do what you feel comfortable doing. Determine for yourself what gauge you need. Each has its own plusses and minuses depending on what you use it for. Guns are for hunting too. That might mean more food in a really bad time, depending on the availability to hunt.

I also recommend you also purchase a handgun. Again, you determine your caliber needs. The shotgun and handgun are really more for defense. You generally don't storm the beach with a shotgun or handgun.

To be more flexible in some disaster scenarios, you might consider expanding this list. If hunting will be important, then buy a hunting rifle that meets your needs for the available game. It might mean a large caliber for moose and elk. It might mean a .22 for squirrels and rabbits. Maybe it will include both. That's what I recommend eventually for everyone anyway. Do it your way though.

Are you are limited in what you can buy, between a shot gun, rifle, or handgun? Then my answer is for you to decide what you want. Weigh all uses for the three types and decide which best fits your needs for the current time. Later you can purchase the additional flexibility of another gun when you can afford to.

Keep in mind a few things I feel are pertinent to the decision. First, a hand gun is never as effective as a shotgun, or even rifles. Second, a rifle or long barrel shotgun can be too clumsy for in a home environment. Third, the shorter hunting shotguns like the Mossberg Turkey Thug can have the camouflage print of a hunting gun, with a full choke short barrel. Thus they are not too clumsy in tight areas like hallways and bathrooms, but are billed as hunting tools as opposed to being a gun nut's tactical weapon.

The one think I hear Jack say more than anything else is that a gun without ammo is just an expensive club. This means you will need to keep a supply of rounds on hand. How much and to what variety will depend on your needs. Have a good supply; probably more than you might think at first, so go buy extra.

One can go a bit further with the defense aspect of prepping. This could include physical fitness and martial arts of sorts. This too is one of those things that benefit us in everyday life. Being fit is good for longevity, and being able to defend yourself might keep you healthy for the near term.

Defense can be rather creative. By this I mean that one can buy crossbows, swords, spears, or other various low tech options. This is particularly of benefit to those in society who might have made bad choices but have been redeemed in the eyes of the law. As you know felons can never own firearms, but bows are another story. It is possible that a redeemed felon will want to defend his family too. Let's give some of them the benefit of the doubt. People do move on from bad choices of the past.

A final thought about bows and other non-firearm related items. These are mostly geared toward hunting, but could be used for protection if really needed. The risk of successfully ending a confrontation with your safety intact is lower. Don't take a knife or bow to a gun fight.

One other thing that is important to self defense is community. Friends and family to cover our backs is defense in numbers. Build a neighborhood network. This does not necessarily mean form a 'watch.' Just make friends and help each other out with neighborly things. If bad times come, they will be there for you and you for them. And if really bad things happen, so much the better. Maybe slowly, they may come to understand the benefit of living a prepper lifestyle. The more people who are ready, the less there will be people who will need desperate help. Remember, prepping is not just for you, it is for us all.

When you need it, defense may be the most important thing you prep for. Think of it as the prepping equivalent to car insurance. You will wish you had it. In some disasters there is a period of time when danger from others is not yet an issue. It takes so many days for someone to become agitated and fearful about the next drink or meal. The longer the time period before help appears, the more desperate people will become.

There is another security choice to discuss; the inclusion of non-lethal defense items. These can be helpful in some circumstances, and not so in others. I recommend that you have some of these tools for the sake of choice. Pepper sprays, tasers, and other typical non-lethal weapons can be easily carried and/or concealed on you. They can be placed at strategic location throughout the home and car too. Check your local and state laws.

I feel the most important reason to include non-lethal items in your gear is their role as a possible legal substitute for lethal force. For example, I carry a handgun and knife while in the Colorado wilderness; sometimes I carry a shotgun. This is for self defense against the possibility of harm by wildlife and other people. I also carry a bear spray canister. This is to give me a level of legal protection in the event I was to kill a bear while out hiking. If a game warden sees that I attempted to preserve the life of the bear, then they will likely be faster to not assume that I am just some yahoo that really prefers killing the government owned wildlife because I thought I could away with it.

This also translates to self defense against people. A prosecutor who tends toward the socialist stance that guns are evil and those who have and use them are evil too; will tend to really push for prosecution of criminal charges even in legitimate self defense cases. Paraphrasing Jack, who always says it brilliantly; this prosecutor will show the jury your tactical rifle or shotgun you shot the intruder with, and say how your buy war weapons and you are this badass who wanted to get into a shootout. But if you have a more traditional rifle or shotgun, they do not have that extra bit of emotional manipulation to use against you and help further their career as the great prosecutor who saves the city from gun nuts.

It will go better for you if you have the non-lethal avenue to try or at least have available. Of course do not go out of your way to show your gracefulness when you are in immediate danger; rather, it is just an available option, but you couldn't get to it. Save you and your family some legal grief and keep this as an option to supplement your safety.

One last strategy for your home's defense as mentioned in chapter 3 is the ownership of dogs. These animals are very effective at securing a territory they feel is theirs and the pack's. When it comes to dogs you and your family members are a part of a dog's pack. They will instinctively act to defend their pack and the area the pack lives in. They add additional awareness to the possibility of defense by their expanded senses. They see, smell, and hear in manners beyond our awareness. They do all this for a meal and a bed. That's a worthwhile trade. In many circumstances the size of the dog will not matter. Most criminals will avoid the noise that little yappers will make. But in more trying times, a big dog or two will really make criminals think better and move on. They do not want to find themselves perforated by inch long teeth that evolved from the bone crushing jaws of wolves.

A successful self defense has many facets to it; choose what is best for you. Just do not be naive to the idea that others might be willing to harm you for something you have or for no reason at all.

Shelter: It's got you covered

Would you go out in the blistering sun in the nude, or a freezing blizzard? No, you wear some sort of clothes appropriate to the occasion. It's the same with having shelter. You live somewhere with a roof, even if it is a shack; at least you have a roof. Some folks don't have even a shack. The homeless know this well enough. They make do with boxes and underpasses. I am sad to see this happening in America, but I can say that they truly do understand what it means to survive.

And survive is what you call it. They may not be where they really want to be, but they meet the first rule of survival. The first rule of survival is waking up breathing each day. They go far in how they do this. They scavenge for food in dumpsters, transport their world in a cart, and live in a box under a bridge. Probably the only thing that makes it bearable is the fact that they can make a box into a home. Something they can call theirs. That is the only foothold they have in staying human.

I see on the news how so many families lose homes in weather related disasters. Some never get to go back to rebuild, some never recover and end up among the long term homeless. I myself could have been in the same boat due to other causes. I count my blessings. I'm sure you do too.

I have seen so many families lose homes due to the financial collapse of 2008-2009. The causes for that could have been prevented on many levels. Greed, fraud, and irresponsibility were the major instigators to that collapse. In hindsight we should not have allowed our nation's leaders to cancel the Glass-Steagall act of 1933, nor allow the investment banks to invent new investment devices based on false debt instruments. For ourselves, we should have had better sense when purchasing homes that were beyond our affordability and living in debt. There is lots of blame to pass around to everyone.

With all that in mind, we still need a home of some sort. Be it a rental unit or one we slowly pay-off, home is where the heart is. Depending on the disaster, we need to plan for the possibility of losing a home. A flood drains away, but is it wise to rebuild in the same spot? Tornados are unpredictable, but less certain to cause us to leave and not rebuild. Bankruptcy happens, but it can be avoided in many cases. Hurricanes, job loss, and spousal death are other common reasons for the loss of a home. Lose an income and you can no longer afford the home, unless you had the foresight to have insurance enough to take care of that and more.

You need options for this basic need. The quality of these options is more dependent on your income than any other basic need for life. I will say it flat out; it is best for you to have a second home of some sort, away from the first one, far away. For some this may never happen; well blessed are those it can happen for.

First, I want to focus on the options available for those who cannot afford a second home in the mountains or on the beach. But first, let's talk money. Maybe you could afford something additional, if you use sound financial habits. Many Americans could afford a second option if they were not living in a house that is already bigger than their true needs. Do not over buy a house. I say live in a smaller and/or older home. This way you have lesser costs going into said home. Smaller homes mean lower monthly mortgages, lower energy bills, and lower taxes. One can save a lot of money in those three areas. Go as far as to choose a home in a low cost area in town, or even a low cost state to live in. For example, Arkansas is a much cheaper place to live in; if you can find work there that fits your job choice. Arkansas has no state income tax to boot, thus you can save even more money. Utah has the least expensive homes on the market. Sound money management in relation to home choice can play a big part in allowing folks to afford more options. Before you consider these options I discuss, get your finances in order.

I recommend a second living location at least 2 hours from where you are. It is up to you to determine how far to go from there. To keep this particular discussion simple, I will treat this discussion as though we do not have to consider distance.

Buy some sort of towable or movable home. If you have to leave, leave in style in a fifth wheel or RV. This can be more affordable than a second home. I have a pop-up camper that has electricity and running water, it cost me $130. Is that cheap enough for your peace of mind? This gives you the option of taking the family somewhere safe ahead of time.

An additional option that builds upon the whole RV thing; is you owning a small tract of land that you can take your mobile home to. Land can be quite affordable in rural areas. Adding to the land owning option is building a cabin. This cabin can be a shed or small building you can live in for hunting. Its affordably becomes a great secondary home site in the event of serious disaster. You can still bring a camper to expand living space. I want to go one step further and recommend that you not keep your RV or trailer at your residence. It does cost money to store them, but there is no sense in losing your trailer to the same tornado that takes out your home.

What I have described above is what is commonly referred to as a Bug-Out Location. A BOL is just a place you can go to in the event you need to leave town. It can be with family or friends. Keep in mind that extended stays with such people can lead to stressful circumstances as the stay gets longer and begins to make them feel imposed upon, unintentionally. It happens sometimes, even though it is not planned on. It is better to plan for the long-term and have your own place for such times. Get into a position financially to do it.

If these cheaper options are not available, and will not be available even in the long run, you still have options. Save a little money for the purposes of leaving town. Keep in mind the need for the other survival needs, food, water, etc. Stay in a cheap hotel. This is not a long term solution, but it will work for very short events. I recommend that you go stay with someone willing to let you, if hotels are not an option for you financially.

For those who can afford a second home, be sure you choose land that is spacious and usable. I will go as far as to recommend it be styled as a homestead location, so if it needed to be, you could keep yourself flexible. One never knows if one might need to go somewhere that they can grow and raise food. This second home will be lived in for some portion of the year I imagine. It will need to be set up so as you can continue your preparation lifestyle there. It too will need to be able to meet all your basic survival needs. Maybe it can become your primary residence in the long run after you develop a plan to allow an income to sustain it.

Energy runs your world

Energy is another way of saying power, though it is not limited to electricity. It can mean animal power or even fire. Whatever can get you heat or a battery charge, power is essential to comfortable living in times of hardship. I want to live as comfortable and as normal as I can, even in times after a disaster.

Depending on the seasons and your geographical location, the need for climate control can be life saving. Having a second location to go to will help in this regard if it has modern conveniences or even its own power sources. This is not an option for everyone, but hopefully a realistic goal. Heating can be more easily provided than cooling. This can be done with even something as low tech as a camp fire. If your BOL is not on the grid, then a wood stove will be a great tool to provide heat within a bug out shed or structure. Some campers and RV have heaters and even air conditioning.

RVs and such also have battery systems and generators depending on its size and upfront expense. These will only last for so long though. Eventually you run out of fuel or charge or both. One can then consider adding solar and wind power production to your BOL or trailer. This is best case for those who can afford that option. For those who cannot go that route immediately, maybe you can go piecemeal.

By this I mean for you to start out with a single car battery charger and controller unit, a deep cycle battery, and a power inverter. With these three items one can make a small battery bank that can later be expanded. With a three stage automotive charger one can recharge a battery at will (as long as power is available at your primary or BOL.) Hook an inverter to it and you have AC power. This can be built into a specified area of the home or BOL shelter. Wire it into the home's electrical system for constant charging or put it in the toolbox in the back of your truck. Then it is mobile and more flexible. For off grid locations or power down events expand you reserve of power by adding batteries one or two at a time. Increase charging by adding solar panels a few at a time.

Please keep in mind that this small of a system will not power an air conditioner or heater for more than a few minutes. It is more for the use of small items that need power. Lights will last a while, especially LED lighting. LED TVs, radios, DVDs, cell phone chargers, or other minor conveniences will make life better. Your living standard will improve with the more the better concept: The more batteries the better; the same with solar panels or a small wind turbine. Start small, thus teaching yourself how to make a self charging battery backup system. Like I said, one charger, battery, and inverter will be easy to put together and use. Doing this will give you the foundational skills to make a larger system later. When you see a set of solar panels on a rooftop, you are looking at an expanded version of this system: Charger, battery, inverter.

If you pull a trailer with a truck it can be built into your truck's toolbox and wired to be charged from its alternator. For more power to any of these types of systems, add a second inverter that has even greater capacity. For trailers and RVs one can only store so many batteries and panels. This little system can only go so far for you and you will have to expand in other ways if you do not have a 2nd home or location where you can place panels for expanded production. For homes and such, this system is not really limited except by finances and expansion room. You can have all the batteries you want as long as you can efficiently charge them. Steven can give you any details you could want on his website.

Above I mentioned fire. The best source of cheap heating in a disaster is wood sourced heat. This depends on several things, including legality. It might not be legal for you to build a campfire in a tornado ravaged neighborhood, or even where a hurricane destroyed your town. The police and other first responders will not let you live there anyway. At a BOL though, you can have campfires if it is in a rural environment. Having a woodstove at the home or shelter will keep you warm if your place has plenty of trees. Staying warm without fire as an option can be done with the battery system and an efficient electric blanket if all else fails. Firewood is pretty much free in the woods, except for the sweat involved in getting it.

Most likely the need for such will not be long term. After all, I am discussing temporary disasters, not the end of the world. Weather events will drive you away from your primary location only for a short time: Days to months. This could even be during mild times of the year. Pretty much camping equipment will provide all you need. Just as a small battery system as described before, a camp stove or wood stove will be a means of providing basic energy for cooking for shorter durations. For very long times of relocation, a change in life is in order.

You might not be able to go back and rebuild. Wars are the most common cause of permanent home loss, but landform changes do occur. There are people in Hawaii who have lost homes and could not go back. Rivers and coasts change shape and your land may not even be there. I cannot offer the solutions to these circumstances, but having a plan for such is a good idea, if it can even be afforded.

Some other sources of power for your convenience that are portable and compatible with bugging out but are still useful for the everyday home are small batteries like AAA, AA, C, and D cells. The best are rechargeable batteries. Charge them from the grid, or use your small battery backup system to plug the charge unit into. They will power headlamps, lanterns, radios, and other useful items. Be sure to have plenty of each variety on hand, most certainly the sizes you use already.

Staying cool in locations without a source of electricity is harder and not very easily rectified; one will need to get rather creative with the laws of nature. Your BOL will need shady places. If you have a building that is not on the grid, the building should be built where shade is covering it during the warmest times of the day. One can utilize evaporation if water sources are plentiful. Open the windows and hang wet sheets. The air will flow through the damp, thin cloth and evaporate the water making a primitive cooling system. Small fans can add to this as long as you build the small battery system I keep mentioning from before. If you have adequate power production or supply, you can purchase AC units that are window mounted or portable like a typical space heater.

Your needs for power will depend on the flexibility of your plan and your finances. In a disaster, everybody's needs are different as much as they are the same. How you meet these needs is your prerogative. Think through what it is you need to do to make it through a power outage. What will you need if you have to flee a city to a BOL? Will your BOL have the ability to meet these needs by default (grid tied) or not? Even if you do not have to leave, will your primary location have the ability to provide your need during longer outages? Worst case, can you live without the power company if you have a situation similar to the unfortunates who lived without power for a month in Hurricane Sandy?

Try living without electricity for even one hour. Go and hit the main breaker to your home. What do you need after ten minutes? Thirty minutes? By the end of the hour, what are you in need of? This is a way to start experimenting with what you need to live through power loss. Repeat it again at a later time; this time extending to half a day. What do you notice that goes wrong? Thinking of your food? Ok, now we are getting somewhere. You need to preserve your food from spoiling.

If it goes bad, you wasted a lot of money. Maybe storing a few large and thick blankets for covering the freezer and fridge would be helpful. Cheap too; you can buy them at goodwill and put them in a tub up in the attic. When power goes out, cover the units and now you have just extended the insulation capacity for the appliances.

Some of your needs will not show up until longer timeframes occur. Test your ability to weather an outage by doing it for a day or two. Simulate the real thing and determine what you can actually do to make any power loss not be such a nuisance. You have heard the stories of the family that has the TV on during the outage, and is acting like nothing is going on. They thought ahead and determined that they would not be too inconvenienced by an outage. This will only go so far though. Being in a hurricane and losing power is not the same as losing power due to some power maintenance guy changing a fuse and knocking out power for two days.

Personally, I will want to be in some level of comfort during a power loss. I might have a generator running, or I might have a full home solar set-up. Maybe I run my car off and on and plug stuff into an inverter. Doing something basic is a first step, doing something big and complex is better, but you have to decide your needs or wants in this situation. What level of power provision is comfortable to you?

Discussed in the shelter chapter were alternative home power systems such as solar, but geothermal, hydro, and wind, though very costly will make your grid tied home work without the grid, or enable you to make your bug out location or homestead be independent and off-grid.

As discussed in chapter 3, you will need fuel for transport, power, and heat. The fuel storage plan discussed there is a stepping stone to other bigger and longer term preparations. Petroleum fuels can be stored in larger quantities if done properly (legally). Large tanks set up to feed a whole home generator can be placed near the home. So can other fuels such as fuel oil and propane. Homes and their backup systems can be set up to run on either of these in any weather or disaster event.

Natural gas is a great option too. In many events the supply will continue to run as long as there are not any breaks in the lines. Wellhead pressures are what run the networks, not power from the local electric companies. A natural gas capable generator wired into the panel box properly will run your home and meet your power needs. You choose whether it is whole home or smaller.

Natural gas opens up another area in which you can increase the flexibility of your personal transport. Natural gas fueled vehicles can then be refilled at home with the proper attachments, though they are very costly.

By the way, a truck can be set up to run on wood gas systems; chop your fuel down. Vehicles can run on propane too. If you have a home propane system, refuel your car at home or stop by Wally World and buy a 20 lb propane tank to plug in. Again I give credit to the person who really came up with this concept; Steven.

Self Reliance is a lifestyle

After the first chapters, hopefully you have come to the understanding that prepping is not something only paranoid people do, but rather something that everyone should do to some degree. All the prior arguments for prepping I have just gone through would be good reasons for all citizens of the whole world to start a prepping plan.

Many people all through the world live a prepping lifestyle to some degree or another already. They would not call it prepping but living. They have no choice in the matter due to the local economy, culture, national economy and politics, wars, weather, climate and so many other reasons for providing themselves with a means to continue in their lifestyle. In some places they already live as though they cannot get food, water, and electricity from a centralized source.

We in the civilized nations should live a lifestyle that at the very least acknowledges that some of our centralized systems of provision may not work as fully intended or at all because of some event or events that these systems are not prepared to function through. It can happen, and it has happened: An important consideration to bring up here its how we can survive through what ever hardships come our way, and rebuild. Life goes on.

What I'm trying to say is that we need more than stuff to be able to successfully be a prepared people. We need skills. Skills such as the ability to build, garden, hunt, repair, and medicate. These are not the only skills or trades that one could use. There are so many, and they are only limited by the imagination of people. New skills and trades are often created as time and knowledge marches on.

We will always need someone who can build something, repair things, grow food, raise animals, and heal people and whatever else society decides is useful to our lifestyles. One man is no island, and they should not expect to be able to know all things. But groups of people can build a community and lean on each other for needs. We do this already in the marketplace. Needs dictate what people learn to provide the rest of us. We need engineers if we wish to build buildings and bridges. We need someone skilled at running merchandise sales. We need people who can provide textiles. The list goes on.

The problem that can arise is revealed when times go bad or something happens to slow or stop this process. If a war were to happen in Brazil and they stopped shipping fruits and veggies, then how many people will be going hungry because we cannot provide some of our own until we find a more secure source of food. The US imports so much food at this point in time; what kind of supply problems would result if the importation is disrupted? In this case it is important that we can have local sources of food provision. This is just one example of how skills are beneficial, especially to a prepping minded individual or group.

I am not saying to join some commune type of group in which you give up all your personal property for the group, unless that is what you want. I am thinking more along the lines of forming a community with your friends and neighbors in your neighborhood or town. If they have a skill that you do not have, maybe you have skills they do not have. It is no different than purchasing or bartering items you need. You grow food, they have chickens. You raise worms, they are good at fishing. This is an easy way to form a community through needs and excesses.

So go out and learn some skills or trades. You don't have to learn them all, just what interests you. Encourage others in your community to learn the same ones or other skills that you do not have. Branch out and get creative, this can also lead to a money making skill to supplement or eventually replace your income; maybe it is already your main source of income. Being resilient in your finances will put you in a better place in the event of economic hard times; and in times of plenty, one can make money on the side. This would mean you are building a means to be even more self-reliant than before.

There is a new and growing trend in our society today centered on good food. As is common knowledge, our modern convenience foods are leading more and more people into lives of sickness and poor living. The trend is such that people are changing the sources of the food they eat. More people are seeking local foods from people that they have more reason to trust. People are buying meats and plant foods that are not raised and processed for the sake of profit, but rather health.

This is happening because people are sick of bad foods that risk contamination by chemicals or biological exposure. They are finding that there are not so many sources to meet this changing market. They end up deciding to try providing some portion of their own food production. This starts out as small to large gardens, a single chicken or a flock, and it turns out to be a success. They grow their operation and find that others want their foods. They sell it and it grows into a local, organic food production income. They went out and learned the skill of raising plants and animals for their own benefit and discovered the potential to make an income.

The possession of skills beyond what you learned for your day to day job will benefit you and your family. Any skills can lead you to a life of less dependence and greater independence. When you are self reliant, you are free. In the case of food skills, you are freed from the sentence of a life of bad nutrition and health. You are free from the poor quality foods that are making Americans and other western cultures, *Fat, Sick, and Nearly Dead*. Other skills might set you free from the corporate slave mines profiteering off your hard work.

There are so many sources from which one can learn to do something. YouTube has many videos that show you how to do stuff. Another source is Google; type "how to" and then what you need to know about, and you will get many links to learn from. Amazon has cheap kindle books to read and learn from, as well as free books too. Instead of wasting time watching useless TV shows, go on the internet, take a class, or go to the library.

Go learn something rather than waste time watching pointless TV all day. I learned to write and publish. I did this by choosing to write over watching TV and feeling sorry for myself. I learned about prepping and wrote a book for you to learn from. In learning about prepping, I learned to garden. I will learn about raising chickens soon. What will you learn that will make your life better?

Debt kills the future, savings saves it

I listened very attentively to my favorite podcasting prepper show the first time he gave a definition of "mortgage." He basically said that *mort-* means death, and *-gage* means grip. So a mortgage is a death grip on whom; you and me?

I have worked toward staying debt free as often as I can be. Sometimes I have to make a car purchase, but I strive to pay it off fast. I make sure that I am not upside-down in my car payment because I just had to get a new car so I could feel good about myself. I learned that by the time I traded in my third car and went into debt for the greatest amount I ever had to pay off. I was not happy for the next five years. I eventually paid it off, and when I purchase my next vehicle it will be used, and I will pay a big down payment. I cannot avoid debt due to my income, but I can loosen its *death grip* on me as much as I can.

You see, I find myself in actual need of a truck due to my new lifestyle of prepping and Colorado vacationing. My new lifestyle does not have room for a Mustang. I cannot take it on mountain trails and I cannot carry my garden supplies in it. Unfortunately I have a meager income and will have to go into debt. BUT I WILL NOT BE A SLAVE TO IT FOR ANY MORE THAN I HAVE TO BE! I am choosing out of necessity, not want.

Understand this, as much as I hate debt, I will use it if I have to. Take the same approach for yourself. Hate it and use it only if absolutely unavoidable. Homes are another debt that cannot be avoided by most people. I say, be wise and careful. Plan it carefully, and purchase what you need not what HGTV makes you wish for. Have a plan to pay it faster than the holder would prefer.

Debt will kill your finances and your peace. Maybe you know this right now. Maybe you know this because you are now free from it. Whatever your case, you know it kills you. The future obligation of debt service and its interest can lead to many things. One thing it leads to is lesser purchasing power for needs that come up. Your water heater busts, floods the house, and the insurance says you do not have flood insurance; your up a creek. If you are making two car payments, a big house payment, payments on the kids braces, and have an overcharged credit card; how are you ever going to get ahead?

Debt guru Dave Ramsey has a most effective program to get out of debt. Go get out of debt, and then come back here to learn to live by a prepping framework. You cannot prep for anything if you cannot buy the small things that get you started. Debt will suck the life from you for years, even while you are successfully paying it down. You are always its prisoner until every last bit is paid and gone. Then you will seek to never have it again, even if it is needed. That's OK, you decide how to use or not use debt. My way is for me, maybe not for you.

Beyond debt is the practice of other positive financial habits. Disciplining yourself to resist impulse buys and other useless purchases that end up getting thrown out will help with keeping you out of debt. I waste so much money on crap that I make myself sick sometimes. Even more so it will help you avoid the feelings related to wondering where your money goes every paycheck. More people in America live paycheck to paycheck than ever before. There are so many things out there competing for your money. Add to that the cultural pressures of having the latest car, home improvements, gadgets, etc; and your money goes pretty fast.

Do you really need to eat out every night, or have that pricey cup of Joe? Change your spending habits and you will have more money for when you really need it. I acknowledge that this can be hard. The first step is to just make a list of things you buy in a given month and then decide what you can live without. Maybe you start with eliminating one item, maybe more. This is your plan; you know what you can do at what pace you need. Just have a willingness to make changes and do them slowly.

This subject is only touched on in my book because there are so many others who write on how to get free of debt's *death grip*. My only focus is to let you know how its absence will let you build yourself into a self reliant person or family. Get debt free and let your money help you build security for bad times. People in debt, even with BMWs and 5000 square foot homes will be as bad off in disasters as a poor people who can never afford a home and are living life off of government subsidies.

Another sound financial habit is saving money and investing it.

Investing money is a whole other ballgame. It is hard enough to just keep what you have, but how do you decide what to do to make it grow. Slow and steady is the only sure way, but the deck is stacked against you by government and banking people.

The government, like any person can be, is greedy for its share of your work, through taxes. The government leverages us for its own interests. The more money it gets from you and I the more it can invent ways of impeding your liberties. What other motive do they have? We all have to pay for a permit to have a garage sale. The most free nation in the world, and we can get fined for not paying the government its fee for us to sell the used junk we want to get rid of.

"It's only five dollars" whines the sheep who doesn't understand. All it takes is some busybody to think that they need more money for the town and see people cashing in at home to think that they need to get a piece of the action, your action. All fees, licenses, permits, and whatever they charge, so you can do it is one way government stacks the deck against you. This reminds me of a protection racket in Chicago gangland. You make the money and we will protect you from whatever if you give it to us too, or we will kill you. I hope you get my real point here.

At this point in the book I will act as though you are in a now of a mind in which you are debt free, and ready to invest your extra money. If you are not debt free yet, take a moment to day dream a little about it. Many people find themselves wondering what to do with the money they now have since it is no longer going into the pockets of rich lenders. They kind of feel a bit weird about having it and not sending it off.

The first things most people do is go splurge and buy a new car or something else. Don't do that, or you will be back where you started. Instead sit down and thing of a small thing you would like to have or do. Don't go crazy and blow it because you like the feeling of purchasing power. Yeah, some people feel more fulfilled just because they have a bit of cash and need to satisfy some emotional void.

If you must, make it a small hobby related purchase or a home repair, or take a short trip somewhere to relax. Think of others and make a donation or some such purchase for another person. Now that that is out of the way, on the next paycheck you can start your savings plan. Keep in mind that this is how I do things. Make it your plan too if you like it, but if not, change it around so it is more compatible with your lifestyle.

First, make a list of your bills and other recurring monthly expenses. Next, make a list of other things that have happened unexpectedly or less recurring than once a month. Third, add up all insurance deductibles as though they suddenly all wanted them right now. Last, select a number between 5k and 20k; this will be the amount of cash you keep in various saving instruments.

The first list is an exact dollar amount of your monthly bills. You may include other forms of bills like car insurance and divide them into a monthly payment or lump them into the next list. Let's say all you bills add up to $1500 for any given month. Take that and multiply it times six. You get $9000. This is you first savings goal to keep in an interest bearing checking account that is not your everyday checking account. Lock the checks away in a fire-rated safe. You can also put this money in an envelope at home if you wish, but in a fire-rated safe, just in case. Now you have the security of six months of bills in the event of something happening to your income. The most important thing here is that you make this a stash you do not use, ever. This is for the event of a job loss or something else.

The second list is a list of other bills and expenses that come up both predictably and unpredictably. Maybe you lump your six month car insurance bill here, or your property taxes, maybe even your income taxes. This is only for items that you pay once a year or more, but less than monthly. I say double it so you have two years worth of this in the same secondary checking account as your six months of bills. I really recommend an account because it will help you not sneak to the safe so you can go buy the winch for the jeep or that really cool rifle. It helps with discipline. Again I remind you that this is not money for this year's bills, but only for the event of a job loss. You are saving your extra money for these lists I am discussing here.

The third list is all deductibles that can crop up in a given year. You will only need one year's worth, unless you want two. The likelihood of spending this is small. Put this into a separate savings account that earns a small interest payment. Every bit helps in the end, right?

The last amount depends on what you feel comfortable with keeping on hand. You can keep it in a home fire-rated safe, or in a bank. I recommend a bank for at least some of it. Let's say you choose $10k. This is the amount of cash you will keep on hand for quick access. This is emergency money that is more for big emergencies that do not recur through a given year. As these emergencies come up you may feel like replacing this cash. Or maybe you decide not to ever use this for even broken down cars. You decide. Take this money and split it into four groups or more depending on amounts larger than 10k. Take one group and keep it at home in your <u>fire-rated</u> safe, then the next and put it into a one year CD, take the third and put it in a two year CD, take the fourth and put it in a three year CD. Now you have immediate access to the first, and less so but recurring access to the rest. As each CD comes up for renewal you renew that one for three years. Now once a year you have a CD coming due for you to decide if you need the money.

This can be scaled up or down in time of renewal, like six months, twelve months, and eighteen months. You can choose a greater or lesser amount of money like 5k or 20k. This is depending on your needs and wishes.

According to this little plan here, which I learned from Jack, and changed to fit my finances, you have the potential to pay all bills, expenses and other big emergencies for six months or more. How you save this is up to you. You can set a goal and save a portion of each for each paycheck until the goal is met. Maybe you save 500 bucks each month to put into each a little at a time. Or you can pick one list and save for them one at a time. You can even add lists to save for. This is your emergency money and is not to be used for any bills ever, unless it is time to delve into the emergency accounts.

So far I have discussed the savings. Now let's talk about investing. This is the hard part, because there is the chance for so much to go wrong, resulting in loss of principles. I will tell you my plan and you decide to make whatever changes you like.

First off, I believe some pretty bad things will be occurring to the US economy sooner or later. With more than a trillion dollars in deficits being added to the national debt every year, I see the dollar losing its value in the long run, maybe even the short run. I also see the dollar losing its reserve status as the world's medium of economic exchange. More countries are beginning to question why they need to buy US Dollars to trade with other nations. India wants oil from Saudi Arabia, SA wants gold from India. They have to go buy US Dollars to make the trade with each other. Well, why? Why not just trade directly? Because, the US will punish them if they skip the US's monopoly on trade, which requires the US to lend them money for a fee (interest) in order to trade for stuff. Well not any more, other nations are realizing that with such deficits, the US cannot afford to enforce this anymore.

What will happen? Our Dollar will inflate, become worthless in the eyes of other nations, and will cause our economy to tank for a while, maybe a long while, maybe like Japan, for a real long time. That means stock portfolios will be very risky.

I cannot advise you more than just be aware of the big risk heading our way. I think it will be risky to put large sums into stock portfolios. I say large because I will put small amounts in, somewhere. I cannot tell where and neither can you. So invest in the typical paper investments that always take a beating at your own risk. There are other options though.

Alternative investments

There are other ways to invest and grow money beside the traditional stock route. There is property and land, precious metals, material goods, skills, and business ownership. Each of these is time tested and proven. Only, don't think you will get rich off these things, because generally you don't. If your goal is to get rich, than read elsewhere, because I am only writing about possibilities and ways to keep your wealth.

Property is my first means of alternate investing. It is common enough throughout the world, but most people do not do it with disaster preparedness in mind. Who in their right mind would own a piece of rural land to go live on in case something bad happens? If a Jew in Germany had land in England, might he have had a better go at it? You can't predict what and when anything might or might not happen.

But from my reasoning in chapter seven, it might be a good idea for some people. So buy some land, hold it for a while, invest in its improvement, maybe sell it, pass it down, or do it again. In twenty years maybe you live on it for a few months, vacation at it, farm on it, or improve it and sell it. You choose, just do something.

Precious metals can be a great investment if you do not take the attitude of many survivalists. By this I mean that if the economy crashes, your gold will not make you rich, it will hold your value in its investment relative to the economy. The manipulative forces that are inflating our currency know where it will lead, they will be ready, and they will know that you will be too. They will profit from it at your expense one way or another.

So I do not invest in gold, silver, and other such things because I expect to get rich and retire. You should not either. I invest because it will make me more flexible during hard times, and if things stay well, I will get at least something from it in the long run. What kind of gold and silver should you invest in?

Not collectible, but intrinsic. By this I mean you should invest in the value based on the spot price of metals, not some made up value because someone says it is valuable due to some error, limitation, or circulation status. Is there a place for such investing? Yes, but as an addition to metals investing, not the sole manner of investment. Keep a few MS-1000 coins, but do not make them the majority of your stake.

My recommendation is to invest in rounds, small ingots, and currency coinage. They are common, well recognized, and easily tradable. Plus, they are not as easily tracked and taxed as stocks, and paychecks.

In addition to metals there are other material investments that can bring you growth in value directly or indirectly through trade. Survivalists often brag about how they are stockpiling bullets for trade when the world ends; or how they are holding gold and silver to buy other things when the world ends. Ok, these guys are kind of nutty, but there is some truth behind their ideas.

Think about what will be needed by people during and after disasters and economic collapses. Food, water, shelter, security, electricity, gasoline, medical care, and so on. What are these 'so on' items? Clothes, shoes, toothpaste, soap, candy, bullets, beer, smokes, and so on. Anything that is used in daily life can become an item that will be sorely missed if someone does not have access to the said items.

During and after disasters, the world, or your area might not be so blown apart that a barter economy will develop into the way of life for however long society can stay together. It might come to that, but it is not likely that one of the world ending disasters that will cause such a thing will occur. Don't get caught up in the doomsday scenarios.

That being said, it might come down to bartering for a little while. It can happen, and if it does, you will want to have something on hand. So make a small investment in a variety of stuff. I recommend that this variety consist of things you use everyday anyway. Food and water will be in demand more than anything else. Especially if the stores are closed, destroyed, or even ransacked

Choose items that fit with your skills, especially if you are a nurse, doctor, or EMT. Be charitable with some folks; be kind of profitable with others. Eventually things will settle down to where it will no longer be necessary to be charitable and maybe you can make a small living until things improve.

I say be charitable because you will be living near these folks during the duration; unless you bug out. Be a neighbor, and help those around you. Maybe they can help you back. Otherwise you might make an enemy and they might get so desperate that they will want to rob you. You will have to defend yourself if it comes to that, and maybe you do so successfully, or maybe you don't.

Do not take the chance; is making enemies and possibly dying or losing loved ones worth being selfish and not kind to those around you? Survival is better in numbers; even wildebeests know this, so you should too. Make friends, but make even better friends when you come to their aid and share or trade. Then you can look after each other when a real threat comes from the other side of town, such as gangs and crime lords.

You can really make a difference with food and water. Plan ahead and store stuff that maybe is really cheap, but you would not eat. Buckets of long term rice and beans will do this. When a neighbor comes give them a scoop of rice and beans. "This is all I can spare, today. Come back next week and I might have found more I will share with you; keep it quiet though or I might not have any for you."

If you have a farm or garden, share that too, and teach them to plant. Teach them even before the hard time begins. Of course in a hurricane, the garden might be destroyed, but help will come in time. In an economic collapse, a garden will be for the long term.

The next ideal investment is in skills, or knowledge. Knowledge can be leveraged for profit and income. Take a doctor for example; they really invest themselves deep in debt to learn medicine for the big potential payout as a lifetime career. You already did the same if you attended college and use your education. You can go and learn additional skills and trades beyond what you learned in your teens and twenties.

I am planning on going to get an EMT certification, learn more automotive repair skills, and gardening skills. I will learn for the rest of my life, and I plan on learning things that will make my life better and more profitable. Choose something to learn about too. You already are by reading this book and listening to my favorite survival guy. Just remember, learning that costs money is a form of investment too.

The final alternative investment I will discuss for this manual is self employment. That too is an investment. That is what business minded folks invest much of their savings into, a career that they control to some degree, and make a living of their investment. Do you have a skill or trade? Turn it into an income stream. In time it might make you a living if times are bad, or not.

When the economy is good or bad, people make livings off their skills. They take their savings and buy tools or other equipment that will enable them to do the business they want to do. Some even go as far as inventing something or building things others want. They provide services and goods in exchange for a living. Maybe you can invest in a business and make a living.

Thoughts concerning health

In the game of survival the first rule is to survive; in other words, to wake up every day. If you get sick or injured during a disaster, the longer that outside help takes to arrive, the more likely you will risk a serious consequence of said sickness or injury. Maintaining the health of those with you and yourself might become one of the most important considerations in a disaster.

The seriousness of this threat requires increasing consideration as the affected area of the disaster increases. A single tornado or neighborhood disaster from a bad storm is not so bad an event in this regard. On the other hand a hurricane that has affected a 1000 mile wide band along the coast is more of a danger. This theoretical tornado might have taken out a doctor's office, an urgent care storefront, maybe a local hospital and maybe one of the local fire station/ambulance dispatches; but, the surrounding towns and counties will respond to any summons of help.

If the hurricane takes out a 1000 mile band of civilization for 500 miles inland, then help from the outside comes from hours and days away rather than minutes to hours. Local help will be so overwhelmed; it might be days before you first hear from them at all, let alone get the medical help for injuries. You are on your own for a bit of time. That will be the reality of the situation, no matter how much you believe that the government should help you. If there is no government, there will be no help.

Now imagine that any and all government services and medical services are out of commission on a greater scale. Really, who wants to think about that? That would be really bad. This can be planned for to a degree.

I advocate for the storage of more than just some emergency kit at your home. I say store a few big tubs of medical supplies. These tubs can be filled with everything in an emergency kit, but to a greater and more useful extent. Band-Aids will not be of much use after a tornado or hurricane, or worse.

What good is having lots of medical supplies if you do not know how to use the more advanced supplies? Get training in the basics such as CPR, and other emergency medical techniques that will save lives if you do use it. This should be one of the first things you do as discussed in chapter 3, but really, it should just be something every American knows anyway. Take the time to invest in this skill.

Any home medical storage should include lots of various bandages and tapes, scissors, bottles of hydrogen peroxide, alcohol, antibiotic ointments, and splints; at the least. Fill it with some over the counter meds and supplies like sulfur and Tylenol. Add other things like white cotton sheets (for additional bandaging), diarrhea meds, cough and cold stuff, nasal rinses, eye rinses, q-tips, artificial skin, burn creams, and whatever else you use and keep on a daily basis.

If you rely on prescription and other related meds and treatments, discuss with your doc the additional prescription back-up to keep on hand at home. If you get a thirty day supply ask to have a sixty instead. This is really important in hurricane zones. The doc might understand if you discuss the results of Katrina with him or her. It was weeks before things were near normal in New Orleans after Katrina. I know some folks suffered and died as a result of lacking their life dependent meds.

Let us not forget the storage of vitamins and other supplements. If things are rough for a long period, and good food is hard to come by, having your supplements will make life more pleasant in an unpleasant time. As an example, take Vitamin C, it will prevent scurvy, and that can show up pretty quick in situations where fresh fruit is not available. So store a variety of supplements too.

As discussed in chapter 5, water will contribute to this if is clean. Have the ability to boil water for consumption and treatment purposes. After all, you cannot get dysentery from boiled water, nor will boiled water be the cause of an infection in some wound you treat.

For the really long term, your storage will run out, unless you are very wealthy and stored a whole lot. Remember though, that the larger and longer a disaster persists, the less likely it is to happen anyway. Only a Coronal Mass Ejection will shut down the world such that help will never arrive, so you do not have to store a five year supply. At the most store maybe a six month supply, which will be less than you think.

Little do most people realize, but they are surviving on a daily basis already. They are doing preventative activities in a daily routine already. They are staying healthy, for the most part. Some are seeking ways to be even healthier. Doing this is a preparedness lifestyle already. They just do not know they are doing preparedness activities.

Remember, the goal is to wake up each day, healthy. People who take vitamins realize that they are not at their full potential. They realize that today's modern industrial food system is deficient in the proper nutrition needs for people to live disease and syndrome free lives. Other than The Survival Podcast and Battery1234, here is my other plug.

As I said earlier, there is a great show called *Fat, Sick, and Nearly Dead.* Give it a chance; it is a documentary, so it can be kind of boring. I want you to notice how the three people the film focuses on are dropping their chemically derived meds and saving their lives and money. I will say now, the purpose of the film is not to get you to decide to lose weight, but rather, to get you to realize certain foods will make you healthy. If you walk away thinking, 'I'm not fat, so I do not need to do this,' you miss the point. Skinny people are also dying from the same things, just from a different beginning point.

Skinny, muscle bound people die from the same diseases and syndromes these guys had. It is not the loss of weight that improved their lives, but the addition of nutrition to their lives. Losing the weight was just a side effect of having the nutrition their bodies were craving. The moment their bodies realized the infusion of nutrients was there, the bodies began to heal on their own. You will watch how these folks changed their lifestyle and learned to live a new and better life.

These people also were able to drop all the toxic medicines they take. Listen to all the side-effects on the commercials for the prescription meds we as a society take. Better nutrition will heal you to better live through a disaster or life event. I recommend juicing and organic food intake. You want to live healthy everyday anyway. If you are sickly, overweight, or a smoker; you will more likely be one of the first to die during the collapse of society and the absence of modern medical procedures.

Food is more that something to keep you alive; it is health, as Plato said "Food is medicine." So when I said it is a good lifestyle to grow a garden so you know what you are feeding yourself, it is a medical thing too. I can safely assume that anyone with Multiple Sclerosis in a hurricane will have a harder time than the guy from the movie I recommended. Having a garden where you grow food organically, storing the same food to some degree, buying organic and healthy food, and eating it daily, is a form of storing medical reserves too.

A great addition to this topic is the array of alternative medicines available to those who seek it out. Another alternative medicine methodology is the Gerson therapy. It has proven to heal cancers and other degenerative diseases. I practice it and I feel it is saving my life. Even the Paleo diet has benefits that can improve your ailments of MS, Arthritis, and Celiacs.

Herbal and other similar alternative treatments can help you live a better life. To some degree, these things can moderate prescription use or even enable you to get rid of it entirely. Proceed with doctor oversight. If you have to find a doctor who is open to this subject, do it.

I hear people say, "You got to die from something." This is stupid, I want to live my life so healthily, that God gets sick of me living so long and healthy, that he decides it is time to take me himself. "Dang, that guy is still alive, ok King Kong, go step on him because that is the only way he will be coming to heaven." I don't want to die from cancer, disease, heart attack, stroke, or any other horrible way to die. I want to die in my sleep because God said I am too old.

Store some health in your body; you never know what the future holds.

Fear: The wrong reason to prepare

There are two schools of thought concerning fear in western culture; the first I will discuss rather shortly if from the secular point of view. I cannot discuss fear from this point of view because I do not know much about it. The second point of view is the biblical view. As a Christian, I feel more knowledgeable about this. So if you are not in agreement with biblical views, read the first bit of this chapter then feel free to skip on. I suggest you read the remainder though because I feel I can give better reasons to not fear things, and maybe you might find I am not here to give a typical sermon on lifestyles.

Fear is a negative thing; it causes panic, bad judgment, and poor results. I never understand why your typical dictators want to rule by the power of fear. The fearful minion might get something done, but it will not be as well done as someone who does things out of devotion. Then they kill the minion for messing up. Go figure.

Fear will mess you up too. In the case of disaster preparation, it will cause you to make bad choices. These bad choices will affect your pocketbook, your relationships, and your sanity in the long run. Do not panic about how much is needed to be done to prepare for the disaster that is coming. What I mean is, do not focus on a disaster that you expect to happen. Do not, for instance, focus on how to prepare for an asteroid hitting the Earth. That is too much for any individual or family to accomplish. There is no way to prepare for the asteroid, especially since you do not know if it will land right on you anyway. If that happens, you are gone no matter how deep you dig.

Do not focus on how you will survive a Coronal Mass Ejection; it is too big and unpredictable. Plus, it is out of your power to do anything anyways. I watched a few episodes of Doomsday Preppers, as you may well have. Each family was preparing for a specific disaster; what if they are wrong. What if a CME hits rather than an asteroid? What if the economy crashed, but they were ready for a nuke to land nearby?

Man this makes me afraid and helpless. Well, why should I prepare for such things if I cannot? "Forget this, I will just succumb to my fear and be the ostrich with my head in the sand." So, fear can cause you to freeze and deny reality. As I said towards the beginning of this book, you cannot prepare for just one thing that might not really happen anyway. Rather, prepare for some minor disasters that happen everywhere already, because one will happen to you eventually. Change your lifestyle to one of flexibility, rather than rigidity.

What's the use anyway? Some might ask this because they do not believe that there is anything beyond our randomly evolved universe full of accidental life. Live while you can then and make the best of it, because there is no hope for something better than now. Read your psychology books, join a group, or try to make things better with positive thoughts. I don't know any more than that. Fear is bad and you can't let your life be lead by it. Makes sense doesn't it?

Now for my own viewpoint; I have learned from my decision to follow biblical precepts as best as I can. Jesus himself, a man who I believe has plenty of documented proof surrounding the reality of his life, says "Fear not for I have overcome the world." What does that mean to a person who believes he is who he claimed to be? Well, I feel that God did create space and time as the Bible says. I feel it to be a literal description. I take everything in the Bible from a literal interpretation. You don't have to agree with me, but I do it because that is the only way the Bible can be taken with consistency in its message.

If Christ is the one who overcame the world then that means that things are taken care of no matter what will happen to me. It also means I can trust him about my life. Christ says, "Do not worry about what you will eat, or what you will wear."

Scripture is full of positive verses, that when you write them on your heart, they will help keep you at peace. A common theme associated with many of the Bible's characters is the amount of peace they feel even when death is at hand. Take Job, he is quoted in The Book of Job as saying, "Though he slays me, I will yet praise him." In Romans it mentions the heroes of faith who did miraculous and great accomplishments, yet in the same paragraph it talks about the faithful who were slain, imprisoned, quartered, beheaded, and other horrible things that we would cringe at. Even today, in many non-Christian nations, Christians are literally jailed, starved, and beaten to death just because of a religious decision.

I believe there is real power in the peace that Christ brings to a person's life when the Spirit of Christ enters them. Paul supports this notion when he says, "...I no longer live, but Christ lives in me... being confident in this, that he who began this good work in me, will carry it on to completion."

If you are a Christian, then you already realize that you alone cannot live in peace and victory over fear, unless Christ is in you. The focus of Christianity is that Jesus, being the only man to ever walk out of his own grave, alive, eating and drinking, and talking with people when they saw him, went to heaven to sit at the right hand side of God. He is both physical man and spiritual God who came to do in us what we cannot do ourselves, if we surrender our hearts to him and trust him.

What this has to do with preparedness and not having fear is straight forward in the Bible. First off fear does not come from God, but is a tool of the devil as he works in the world to make people live lives of chaos. His goal, according to the bible is to "be just like the most high." He wants Gods role, to be over everything. He wants to show all, that his way is better. God is giving him his spotlight for now. But a day will come when Christ returns and squashes the devil and his plans.

Until that day we have to live in the way of this battle as by-standers. It sucks, but that is how it is if the Bible is right. "Fear not for I have overcome the world."I will choose to trust this because not trusting it, not believing it, will not change it if it is true.

2000 years ago Paul wrote a letter to the Thessalonian church in Greece, in which he included a verse about the times before the return of Christ. As we know in Revelations, an anti-Christ will gain control of the world. He has to set up systems and institute chaos to run the world to prepare for this. That means bad times; end of the world stuff. End of the world stuff kind of like what has been scaring people for half a century now. Nuclear war, asteroid hits, global climatic disaster that will kill us all, alien invasion, a world government that will enslave us all, Y2K, the US economy crashing and causing world depression, and China taking over the world.

Will it lead to Revelations? I don't know, but I believe it will. I hope not; but I feel it is going to happen and I might live to see some of it. It will suck if it does happen that way. I can do something to kind of prepare for it. That is one minor reason why I think and live a life of preparedness. But again, I feel more strongly that everyday disasters are more likely to happen in my future lifetime.

In 2nd Thessalonians Paul wrote them to warn them about the future events coinciding with the return of Christ. So they would not be caught unaware. He then says this, "That ye be not shaken in mind, or be troubled, neither by spirit, nor by word, nor by letter as from us, as that the day of Christ is at hand." If one goes to the original Greek wording and translates it into a more fitting English translation, the meanings conveyed by the context of the language is flowing with much better description.

"Some things will be happening right before His coming that could shake you up quite a bit. I'm referring to events that will be so dramatic that they could really leave your head spinning— occurrences of such a serious nature that many people will end up feeling alarmed, panicked, intimidated, and even unnerved! Naturally speaking, these events could nearly drive you over the brink emotionally, putting your nerves on edge and making you fell apprehensive and insecure about life. I wish I could tell you these incidents were going to be just a one-shot deal, but when they finally get rolling, they're going to keep coming and coming, one after another. That's why you have to determine not to be shaken or moved by anything you see or hear. You need to get a grip on your mind and refuse to allow yourselves to be traumatized by these events. If you let these things get to you, it won't be too long until you're a nervous wreck! So decide beforehand that you are not going to give in and allow 'fright' to worm its way into your mind and emotions until it ruins your whole life." ---Quoted from Rick Renner's book *Sparkling Gems from the Greek.*

2000 years ago this man understood human psychology more than 'modern' shrinks who blame our mothers and claim that others are the real cause of our own troubles associated with mental instability. We need to choose not to let ourselves be traumatized by junk in life. Whether it is about the end of the world, or if we have anger at parents or spouses, we have to be mentally tough like these people who faced Nero's outright slaughter of Christians.

The Bible leads all readers to Revelations, which describes days when a fourth of the human population is dead in one judgment or whole oceans of fish are killed. But we are still to be strong minded. When it comes to any world-ending disasters that doomsday prophets are saying are upon us, we need to keep in a state of peace. Get your peace from the Bible, or not, but have peace and strong minds, so you do not go nuts when preparing for a disaster that will come.

The world is flowing in its natural cycles. These include tornadoes, hurricanes, tsunamis, economic crashes, car crashes, dead spouses, and job losses. Store up peace and internal strength so you can survive without trauma induced consequences. Live life, even live it in the middle of a bad disaster.

I will live through some disaster; I will live it in comfort and style as best I can possibly can.

Do you need a bunker?

First go back and read the last two paragraphs of chapter 12, they are just a summary conclusion of the chapter that those who skipped the religious stuff should at least look at. They are not part of the sermon.

For the sake of consistency, I do not think anyone needs a bunker. But I would have one if I could afford it for several reasons. The fact that they make great tornado shelters is the most obvious reason. You can hide them really well so that they can be hidden even in populous areas. The cheapest might be a purpose built tornado shelter, anything else that is to be a true bunker will get very costly if it is manufactured. You can go with a self dug and constructed bunker, if you have the time.

Bury it in your back yard, though all the neighbors will know it is there. You can share with them or not, but that could lead to losing friends the day of the disaster. Obviously its use as a storm shelter is not likely to be thought of as something to not share. But its use as a longer term shelter might lead to problems with neighbors who know of its existence.

Out in the country on the other hand, one can bury a shelter/bunker without anyone's knowledge beyond the installer. If you own land where things are not visible by neighbors, you can bring in the components during the night and have it buried anytime. Give the guys a tip for their night delivery, they work hard.

Let's talk about how to plan your bunker if you do decide to go this route. If you are building a house before you even move there, install the bunker under the house and construct a hidden trapdoor allowing access secretly. The bunker will need a secondary exit. Never depend on a bunker to keep you absolutely safe. They are a *dead* end. Bury concrete sewer tubes to make a tunnel from the second exit point. Seal them real good from leaking and flooding. Try to have it lead downhill from the bunker to assist with drainage. The exit point can be concealed a ways from the house.

If your home is already built, then bury the bunker right next to it with an entrance constructed to attach it to the home from the crawlspace or basement. Otherwise cut the foundation where it is ok to do so and attach it there with a hidden hatch. Remember to put on the second exit. Disguise the digging with a garden bed system on top of it.

Now your bunker can be your primary storage room. How much depends on how many rooms it has, and how the property is situated in the local flood zones. Even a bunker can flood from high water overtopping the air venting. Make the venting sealable and operable for opening and closing. Conceal all air venting in rock or tree trunk disguises, or whatever you fancy. If the venting makes sound, find a way to prevent anyone from hearing it.

Inside the bunker, if it is not threatened by flooding in any way, you can make it into a secondary living zone. It will need running water, electricity, and climate control. Kitchen, bath, and sleeping areas will make life so much better in a bunker. Provide all the necessary essentials to live for a while inside. Maybe you will have the ability to go in and out safely, maybe not. Food, water, guns, and entertainment will add to the extension and safety of your life and happiness. Why not add entertainment?

You will need something to do if you stay inside for any length of time. If you include electricity then add the electrical items you feel you will like to have with you. I have seen fully furnished bunkers that have TV, radio, and internet. Hah, why not?

The provision of electricity can be a danger point. If bad guys know you are there they can cut it and suffocate you out. Certainly if your home is grid tied, then so should your bunker, but if you are not grid tied your alternative energy source can be just as easily cut. A generator is nice, but if bad guys are around they might hear it or keep it from venting right. They might even be able to prevent you from refilling the tank.

A tank can be buried and concealed to a limited degree; the guy who refills it for you has to get his big truck right up to it, so it too can be vulnerable. Now maybe the most safe would be hydro power or geothermal. Both of these can have buried wiring, and disguised mechanics. Especially if the hydro is placed away from the house in any stream nearby that is not visible to the bad guys. So security is not certain but needs to be considered.

A bunker is useful, but costly. Have what you can afford and no more. Do not destroy your financial plans due to the fear that you just got to have a bunker. You don't! If you have to, turn off the darn TV and stop watching the doomsday shows. They are only for ratings and profit, not educational purposes. Yes, you can learn some very good ideas by way of example, but you will also learn the negative fears that these people are consumed with. I bet all my money that these people originally did not have the total fear they have now, when they started the idea of being prepared or self sufficient. They learned their fear from others. Do not learn their fear.

The single event to prepare for

For this chapter, I am entitling it with a phrase that I do not believe in. There is no one single disaster to prepare for. There are too many disasters to prepare for. However, I will touch on a single plan that is adaptable to several disasters that are commonly feared in this manner. No matter how anyone will try to get them to see reasonably, they are too far imprisoned in their fear and obsessive disorder to understand reason, so I give them a bit of planning ideas too. Some people just need to be told what to do; they need a list to follow because they really are not able to think for themselves well enough in this regard. They do work just find in other areas of life, just not here.

The disaster I think fits this type of planning is the 'Economic downfall of the US." This scenario starts with bad times for the American Dollar. This begins with a bad recession like the 2008 debacle becoming something more similar to the depressions of the past; only worse. Worse because the US loses its reserve status, thus weakening the Dollar so much that inflation is the only way to pay all the nations to whom we owe the current 17 trillion Dollar debt. Nations like China, who in 2013 possesses nearly a trillion and a half dollars in our treasuries and bonds. Like Japan who owns around a trillion dollars in those same paper assets of debt.

Eventually nations will begin to decide they no longer need to be tied under our economic imperial laws we enforce with the world's most powerful military. When we became the world's benefactor after WWII, we got to make the rules. We went too far by putting all the world's nations at economic risk when we introduced them to fractional banking, reserve banking, and Dollar based trade. Now we have gone so far as to create a world debt unlike any ever before. Do not forget that we also lead the world in leveraging the debt by 40, 50, 70 times in value. Something from nothing it is called.

This debt is valued not by assets, but by the full faith of the US treasury and government. This full faith is centered around ideas that can change at the drop of a hat, due to lobbyists bribing representatives and appointees into making laws; laws that manipulate and devalue the same debt. Recall when Ben Bernanke admitted to Ron Paul that the Federal Reserve could guarantee the money will be there to pay future debts and unfunded future liabilities such as Medicare and Social Security. He also admitted that he could not guarantee the value of those Dollars.

It's as though Bernanke knew where the Fed's financial plan was taking the Dollar; to a devaluing of the Dollar. We, the tax payers, will have to pay 17 trillion in direct debt owned by many nations who are slowly divesting themselves of it. Add to that the 150 trillion in unfunded liabilities promised to the American people as retirement devices of various sort. The EU has been struggling with ways to avert the debts they have created in the same way. Japan has been for 20 years, China slows down because they are getting paid with funny money, and Iran refuses to add their value to the pie so the ponzi scheme will grow. Only, it will be shrinking as nations like India and Australia wise up and start heading out.

Sooner or later this will complete the circle and come back and haunt us, the American Taxpayer. Nobody will buy our debt at that point. And with all the wasted money the US Government wastes on socialized ideals, which drain money rather than create money; we need fresh infusions of cash from the outside to keep it all going. The only people who will buy US debt will be the US, only to keep it afloat. That will lead to inflation worse than Jimmy Carter's misery index; maybe even hyperinflation to some degree.

So the Dollar becomes so debased that we are in a Greatest Depression with nowhere to go. The fed pays welfare and food stamps with truly funny money. Everyday grocery, gas, electricity, and other basics of the American lifestyle rise in prices, not because they are more valuable, but rather it will require that much more of this trade unit to get them. Well, that will lead to riots and other similar social unrest because nobody can get food. Shelves are always bare, and the truck is always late.

More and more unemployed that cannot buy products to pay the workers; no money to buy a service from lawyers, mechanics, and carpenters. These are just a drop in the bucket for the possibilities of the economic interruptions that will occur. Unrest leads to danger, which means more crime and victims.

In the middle of all this comes the tax income for any level of government. What are they going to do when we cannot buy gas to provide gas tax revenues, or even property tax revenue? Arrest and audit the 40% unemployed? No, they will print more fake money that dilutes the value of all the previously printed pieces of paper. They will cut jobs in the government; cut pensions and social payouts; cut police, medical, and fire services; cut medical care programs, home and school loan programs; and all sorts of programs that the American people will rely on more and more.

Unrest will increase, maybe even lead to local violence seeking to replace government. There are so many groups who actually want to do such. This environment will lead to great amounts of social divisiveness like that leading up to The War Between The States. If law enforcement and other government systems fail or become neutered; then gangs of thugs will have more sway for the duration. How long that lasts is not certain, so what do you do?

First you leave cities and move to a smaller community where folks know each other and help each other. Suburbs are bad choices for this move. Get out at least an hour from even the suburbs. You need to do this now or as soon as you can. Live on a large tract of land of at least two acres. With this amount you can build green houses, gardens, chicken coops, and have a cow or goat.

Another thing to consider in the country is the alternative heating and power sources. You can choose what to do about this. Keep in mind grid tie if you are not too far out, which I think being too far out is a danger because you are lone wolfing. If you have electrically powered water and climate systems, then add to it the ability to supplement it or back it up with solar, wood, or propane heat. You might have enough sustainable wood on your land or in nearby forested areas. Go with wood. You might have the ability to bury a large propane storage tank to run, hot water and heating. Great! Maybe you can do both.

Keep in mind other electricity systems too, such as solar, wind, geothermal, and hydro. They make your homestead so much more flexible in times of hardship and rationing. In the very long run you save money, but for the immediate term you gain freedom from worry and dependency on government regulated/influenced businesses.

You need to have a skill that will be in demand so you can make an income. Skills such as a mechanic, doctor, nurse, handyman, farmer, would have. Skills to build self sufficiency focused projects will be in demand. If you know how to put in a battery back-up system for homes, people will want that for when the power companies cannot provide enough power for everyone at once. Learn to grow plants and livestock; teach others to do the same.

You will need to provide much of our own food to mitigate the escalating prices in stores. Food will not be cheap any more. Get a bike to do errands with around town to save fuel expenses. Do whatever you can to cut costs. Pay off debt as fast as possible regardless of type and size. Especially important to get paid off is school debt; that is debt that you cannot square away with bankruptcy.

In the country, hunting is an excellent source of supplementing your food. Do not depend on it though, because every other yahoo out there who is not good at prepping properly is out there saying that they can just hunt for their food too. You will have lots of competition for the limited amount of game.

Have a local community support group set up. Make as many friends as you can and be generous with those who are also generous. They will have your back in times of need and you had better have theirs too. You will not make it through this as the lone wolf. You got to sleep sometime, and when you do you will not be able to defend and hold that which is yours; make friends.

Store up supplies of cheap food for making friends, but add to those supplies of food for your family. Learn to buy as inexpensively as possible. Teach others to do the same. Also, store medical supplies, extra car parts, and maintenance supplies like oil and filters. Store extra ammo and have guns. Learn how to use the guns too. Maybe you can train others to properly use guns.

This list goes on and on. It is a list of things to do in all disaster situations anyway; with a little tweaking depending on the region of the nation you live in. Live life as close to this on a daily basis and you will be ready for almost any situation. Except world ending disasters; in which I suggest you get a six pack, go on the roof, hug your family, and watch the fireworks.

What f you cannot get out of the urban zones? You will not be alone, but you will be in more danger from the roving unrest. This is another excuse to make sure you are a community minded person. Entire neighborhoods can be organized for the meeting of various needs, such as security and food production. All the same principals apply for those who remain in the city. You will need food, water, security, shelter, and energy. In some ways it might be easier to meet these needs, after all, cities are the resource concentrated zones of today's society.

Most likely, being in a city will put you higher on the services list when services begin to reappear. Cities seem to be a higher priority for rescuers and other similar agencies. Power companies send their repair crews to the most populated areas of an outage first, out laying areas are serviced later.

My preference is the country, but the only person who can decide what is best for you is you. So decide to have a plan for leaving if it is really the only choice, or staying because you really would rather not leave your home and neighborhood. Choose one and go with it with everything you can put into it.

Common natural disasters

There are too many natural disasters that instill fear and panic in the minds of traditional survivalists. As mentioned earlier in this book, I mentioned CMEs, nuclear war, asteroid impacts, climate change, and world domination by an antichrist. These are events that are unrealistic in their likelihood to occur. I advocate preparation for events that will occur; again, events that **WILL** occur.

Tornados, hurricanes, floods, fires, blizzards, earthquakes, volcanoes, job loss, injury, sickness, death, economic downturns, and other similar disasters that hit on a daily basis somewhere in the world every day. These events cannot be predicted, but yet they can be. To a certain degree, we can see them coming.

Natural forces are at work around us every day. They come on a predictable schedule, by way of the weather services, and other government related entities such as the US Geological Service and the National Oceanic and Atmospheric Administration. We can have a heads up and generally know when to seek cover or evacuate. The citizens of New Orleans had ample warning; some wouldn't or couldn't get out. New York City had warning, yet so many people were in denial that NYC would be flooded.

Most of the big regional disasters that occur are best prepared for by having a means to leave and take refuge elsewhere. The first thing to do to be prepared to leave is to have a closet designated for your bug out gear. Have some baggage prepared for every member of your family filled with items that are essential. You, your spouse, each child, the pets, and any additional people living with you need to have clothes, sanitation, medications if so required, and anything that they use on a daily basis they cannot be without. Also have baggage that is essential for all the people in your family; food, water, money, identity and financial documentation, entertainment supplies, lights, batteries, and other similar small items that will make living on the go more tolerable.

If you can afford to, have an RV or camper trailer that is always filled with some of these things. If you have to leave, you can do so at short notice when you have the items already packed and staged. It may not be feasible to keep it all in the trunk of the family car, but have it near at hand in the home, if not in a RV or trailer. Keep the most important bag in the car, rather than all the gear.

Each region will require a different approach to being staged to bug out. In blizzard prone areas, you may not be able to leave, and it would be too cold to sleep in an unheated camper. Tornado alley has its own unique circumstances. You usually will not bug out in a tornado. Keep in mind that tornados are generally small in scope. But if your bug out transport is kept at the house you risk losing it. Maybe you need to keep your trailer or RV at a storage/parking facility on the other side of town. This way you only lose the home, or the RV, not both.

Bugging in is different to bugging out in that your gear is not located for the event of leaving but rather staying. Preparation for bugging in depends on your home. Do you have a basement or storm shelter? Is yours flood resistant or fire resistant? If you have one of these home features, then store much of your gear in it. It is a place for you to enter at the drop of a hat. Due to regional temperatures, you might not want to store perishables in a shelter, but they can be stored in a closet that is closest to the shelter if it is an outdoor shelter. Keep this in mind if you have an RV, as they are also not ideal places to store perishables.

Some disasters you have no choice but to leave. Forest fires, tsunami, floods, and hurricanes all are best approached with an attitude of evacuation. In this case your stored items might be vulnerable to damage because they are in your home. Others like volcanoes and earthquakes might require a delayed evacuation just as likely as a bug in. In some of these the disaster is during the time after the initial event, but this applies the further out you are from the so called epicenter.

Your vulnerability to these disasters can be lessened significantly by a minor relocation. Ideally, it should be your first goal to never own a house in any flood prone area like ocean beaches, rivers, and lake shores, even though these are generally the prettiest places to live. If you have to, then plan ahead by building high and dry as best you can by constructing the home on the highest point or making a earthen high point for the home to be on. Also do not live in a fire danger zone unless you are willing to continually practice fire prevention techniques such as tree trimming. Even the materials your home is made from can improve fire resistance in the event of blazes. Construct your home with stucco and metal roofing, which are very fire resistant.

I also feel it is a really wise person who does not live in a fault zone or near a volcano. If there is really no choice due to family and work related circumstances, then be ready by having a home that is fire resistant and very structurally sound. A home that can resist the gas lines and roof being shaken apart or even the massive weight of volcanic ash will be a better home to bug in at.

Where you choose to live will play a big part in keeping you and yours safe and comfortable. I acknowledge that some of us will live in areas more threatened in one thing or another. Adjust to it as best you can, or be ready to leave. Some of you should make it a point to move, if you can afford to. Make it a long term goal to accomplish over a period of years.

Now, concerning events that are not natural but happen as a result of living in modern times, I feel they are prepared for just as you would for a natural disaster. A job loss, injury, or even death of a spouse is similar to a bug in situation. No matter what happens to decrease your living standard and income, someone will likely continue to live at home and do their everyday activities. The life style of preparedness will mitigate the impact, especially as we discussed it in the food chapter earlier in this book.

Ideally, you are part of a family, or they are nearby. This way you can depend on others to help in some ways, but you will in some other regard not be such burden. Being out of debt, having savings, having extra food, being able to provide some portion of your own food, having frugal habits, and being able to cut off your extras without their being such a hard thing to do; they all contribute to surviving a job loss, injury, or death more resiliently.

Have a realistic plan, to leave if you must, or to stay if it is best. Have a plan to leave after you have remained for a time. Have a plan for when you get to come back home too. Coming back is the time of rebuilding, and that can be a hard time too. Just have a plan that fits your circumstances best; all the while you learn some ideas from me to apply on the time frame you see fit to decide on.

<u>Closing thoughts</u>

In closing I want to repeat a few things. This is not a book of my ideas that I came up with totally on my own but borrowed from others, mostly Jack Spirko. He is an unequaled source of information. Nobody out there can teach, describe, and discuss this topic as he does. Although this book uses many of his ideas and methods, they have been recorded in a manner related to how I am adapting them to my life on an everyday basis and passed on again.

Good luck on your plan; remember to get your mind in check and not react in fear. Go slow, take the time to breath, and just pick one thing to do at a time in each category of need. Start with the basics; have food and water. You have shelter and energy if you live somewhere other than the streets; so after the most important things are met to a minimal degree, then get a means of security.

Nobody can be perfectly prepared; especially overnight. This is a lifestyle change that leads to self reliance in the long term. Do not rush this. Enjoy your everyday lives, or what is the point of living in fear during good times. Remember, it just might be that you will never experience anything worse than a day without power; or you might experience it all at once. Regardless, live your life and choose to be aware and accept that the unpredictable can occur, and you simply want to be on your feet when it does.

Finally, have the attitude that any and everything you do to prepare must be something that will improve your living standards somehow. If it is not an improvement in your lives, don't do it. To do something just for the sake of doing it and it brings no level of peace, it is done in fear. You have no reason to fear anything in the prepping world; you have everything to look forward to because it will make life better; even if a disaster never happens to you or anybody you know.

Return to beginning.

     Thank you for reading my book. If you enjoyed this book, or found it to be informative, please leave a review at the web store you purchased this from. Look for more Dr. Disaster books in the future.

Check out the face book page.

Check out Jack's podcast.

Check out Steven's battery back up page.

4420696R00057

Printed in Great Britain
by Amazon.co.uk, Ltd.,
Marston Gate.